# Light in the Last Days

*Boniface Ossai*

Boniface Ossai

Paperback Edition First Published in the United Kingdom in 2025 by aSys Publishing

**Copyright © Boniface Ossai**

Boniface Ossai has asserted his rights under 'the Copyright Designs and Patents Act 1988' to be identified as the author of this work.

**All rights reserved.**

No part of this book may be reproduced or transmitted in any form or by any means, electronic, mechanical, photocopying, recording, or otherwise, without prior written permission from the Author.

**Disclaimer**

This is a work of fiction. Names, characters, businesses, places, events and incidents are either the products of the author's imagination or used in a fictitious manner. Any resemblance to actual persons, living or dead, or actual events is purely coincidental.

ISBN: 978-1-913438-93-7

# *Dedication*

I lovingly dedicate this book to the memory of my late brothers, Emmanuel and Felix Ossai.

With deep gratitude, I also dedicate it to my beloved wife, Nkem, and our children, Ikechukwu and Ifeanyichukwu, for their unwavering support and encouragement.

Lastly, this book is dedicated to all the saints around the world who endure persecution for the sake of Christ. May your faith continue to shine as a light in the darkness.

# CHAPTER ONE

## *Who is God*

The question of God is something many people never deeply consider in our world today. This is particularly true when our lives are flourishing and when we are solely dependent on the government for our upkeep. The question of God suddenly comes to the forefront of our minds when we realize we are in the sunset of our lives. Research has shown that the three major questions people ask in their dying moments are:

- What happens to me after I die?
- Does heaven really exist?
- I never believed in God; if heaven really exists, will God accept me into heaven?

The truth remains that God is preparing a better place where we will live with Him for eternity. Our actions in this transient world (earth) enable God to filter the good from the bad. He leaves the choice of being good or evil to us, and then the judgment that follows is His. God is intrinsic and cannot be objectively or quantitatively measured. He is an unknown quantity, and He would rather we believe in His almightiness to experience His limitless power than dwell on the extent of His power. God is bigger than the biggest ocean if the ocean is our basis of measurement, and He is taller than the tallest mountain if height and size are our basis of measurement. God dwells in the spirit realm. He created the heavens and the earth, and His relationship with humans is transcendent. God is divine but allows man to relate with Him based on their free will. God is spirit but can interfere with the course of nature, and that is what brings about miracles. God's nature is more about believing in Him to experience His power than experiencing His power to believe.

From the days of Noah and Enoch to the days of Abraham, God has always related to humans on the premise that if they believe in Him, they would experience His power. Noah believed and built the ark before he saw the flood. Abraham believed, and God established him in return. God changed this approach when He needed to rescue the children of Israel from the land of Egypt. He had to adopt a new approach where the Israelites would have to experience His power to believe in Him, which is the reverse of how He had previously related to humans. The Israelites could see the cloud during the day, the pillar of fire at night, and they would know, "That's God right there." This relationship, where the Israelites had to see God in the form of a cloud or pillar of fire, changed the moment they entered the promised land.

God reverted to His former approach, which requires us to believe to experience His power. Joshua understood this very well. With the cloud and pillar of fire gone, faith would be necessary to believe in God. This is why Joshua admonished Israel to choose God, even as he reminded them that he and his family would choose to serve the Lord. Joshua 24:15-17 [NIV]:

"15 And if it is evil in your eyes to serve the Lord, choose this day whom you will serve, whether the gods your fathers served in the region beyond the River, or the gods of the Amorites in whose land you dwell. But as for me and my house, we will serve the Lord." 16 Then the people answered, "Far be it from us that we should forsake the Lord to serve other gods, 17 for it is the Lord our God who brought us and our fathers up from the land of Egypt, out of the house of slavery, and who did those great signs in our sight and preserved us in all the way that we went, and among all the peoples through whom we passed."

Joshua saw the need to admonish the people because, as humans, we have a tendency to forget. The Israelites did hold on to God as Joshua had advised, but over time, they strayed from Him and began worshiping other gods. We all live in a fallen world, and humans by nature are unlikely to do what is good by God's standard. Even as humans demonstrate an inability to get their act together, God has, from generation to generation, remained committed to us, seeking ways to reconcile us to Himself at every opportunity.

Interestingly, Christ came to show us the ways of God and sent the Holy Spirit to help and comfort us. However, the world has strayed further from God, and the children of darkness now openly show their disdain for Him. Therefore, remaining indifferent about our Christian faith at a time when so many people are under the sway of the devil would be like watching the bus driver lose his vision while the bus is still in motion and hiding this from the other passengers. Humans are social animals, and we co-exist through relationships. In the course of our lives, we form strong bonds with friends and loved ones and desire for these relationships to last forever. Sometimes, these relationships are severed unexpectedly due to death, exposing our vulnerability and harshly reminding us that we are ephemeral.

When people grieve, they often ask questions like, "Why did my friend die?" or "Why is there death?" and "Why can't I be happy and not worry about dying someday?" They ask these questions as they try to make sense of a deeply painful and confusing experience, attempting to find some logic or explanation for the loss, even when none may exist. Interestingly, death is not the end of any soul, but a transition. The question then is, "Transition to where?" This is where understanding God's intentions towards man becomes necessary and comforting. RT Kendall recommended two things every human must do: "Know your Bible and pray." If you read your Bible, you will understand the ways of God, and if you pray, you will be led by the Holy Spirit to guide your journey on earth.

# CHAPTER TWO

## *Relative morality*

When God created man, He instructed them to have dominion over everything He has created. This assignment comes with responsibility, accountability, and some level of autonomy, in other words, free will.

God gave man free will, not only to serve as a yardstick for judgment (for deciding those who on their own will choose to serve God or not), but to enable us to live our everyday life as we journey through earth. Free will enables us to make a choice on what clothes to wear, what car to buy, what food to eat, who to associate with, and even who to marry from the many options available to us. However, humans have taken free will to mean more than choosing what to eat or wear, but to be more about whether to serve God or not.

It is increasingly becoming a trend in most conversations in our world today that God isn't a necessity in how we run our lives. Most people today will always argue that they don't need a God to know what is right and what is wrong (like they don't need a God to know that killing is wrong, they don't need God to know that stealing is wrong, or even telling lies is wrong). This view has led those who hate God for one reason or another to encourage lukewarm Christians to abandon the Church.

Therefore, if we don't need God's view on morality to act as our moral compass, we have by implication made ourselves God, deciding for ourselves what is right and what is wrong. Each time I engage people in conversation about the place of God in our lives, and they respond, they don't need a God to know what is morally right and what is morally wrong. I usually observe a sudden retreat when I make them understand they are deifying themselves by assuming the position of God and ask if they can consistently live out their moral views.

Every tribe, people, or nation has explicitly or implicitly acknowledged their connection to God. Regardless of their beliefs or mode of worship, they have, in some way, acknowledged the existence of God.

From the medieval period to the Renaissance and even through the rebirth of medicine from the 14th to the 17th century, it is documented that people worshiped their gods in various forms. From Africans living in the dense forests of Africa, to the Egyptians during the time of the Pharaohs, the Native Americans, the Shamans, the Babylonians, the Greeks, and the Romans, all have worshiped some form of deity. Regardless of the tribe, one thing remains common: the acknowledgment of a supreme deity. We have the Mesopotamian god, "Anu," the Greek "Zeus," the Norse "Odin," the Yoruba people of Nigeria worship "Olorun Olodumare," the Igbos of Nigeria worship "Amadioha," the Pharaohs worshiped "Horus," and the Romans worshiped "Jupiter."

The modes of worship may differ, but they all express a desire to connect to something higher, something beyond the physical realm, their maker. The question remains: how did it come to be that all these people and tribes, from different parts of the earth, came to recognize the need to worship a god, especially at a time when the world wasn't as connected as it is today? We can ask further, where did the insight into the need to worship God come from? This is because there is part of every human being that bears witness to their connection to God. Romans 8:16 [NIV]. "The Spirit himself testifies with our spirit that we are God's children."

Aside from the Bible story when men came together to build the Tower of Babel and God scattered them, there was not a record of any moment in history when all humans on earth had that contact and communication to have come to the acknowledgment that there is a maker. This implies that the illumination on the existence of a maker is intrinsic, coming from within and not passed on by one tribe to another.

Consequently, before Christ, every people and tribe formulated their own ways of communicating with their maker. The question that begs to be answered is: how acceptable is our worship to God? This can be likened to a one-year-old child rushing to hand his toy to his dad the moment he walks through the door after work, or in another case, the child rushing to get his dad a cup of water, thinking he's thirsty and needs a drink. The child is trying to please his father, but he doesn't truly know what his father needs at that moment.

In order to harmonize all these modes of worship into something acceptable, God had to send His son, Jesus, to lead the way and let us know what God truly thinks. From the day of Pentecost, God has done so much, and He continues to ensure that all these different modes of worship, from various tribes, people, and cultures, are brought into alignment with the way He prescribes. God needed to harmonize how humans worship Him, and He did this through the person of Christ. He did this by scattering the disciples and apostles, allowing their persecution, which ultimately led Philip to India.

Many Christians, who think lazily, have resorted to the view that being moral, kind, and doing good works, like engaging in community service, surpasses accepting Christ into our lives. However, God does not accept anything and everything as true worship. Acts 10:1-15 sheds more light on what God expects from us. Cornelius was a centurion, a commander in the Italian Regiment of the Roman military, and most importantly, a Gentile. Cornelius' story is paramount in our world today, not only because it was in Cornelius's household that God publicly opened the doors of the church to the Gentiles, but also because it gives us insight into God's heart toward humanity.

Act 10:3-18 [NIV]. "3 One day at about three in the afternoon he had a vision. He distinctly saw an angel of God, who came to him and said, "Cornelius!" 4 Cornelius stared at him in fear. "What is it, Lord?" he asked. The angel answered, "Your prayers and gifts to the poor have come up as a memorial offering before God. 5 Now send men to Joppa to bring back a man named Simon who is called Peter. 6 He is staying with Simon the tanner, whose house is by the sea. 7 When the angel who spoke to him had gone, Cornelius called two of his servants and a devout soldier who was one of his attendants. 8 He told them everything that had happened and sent them to Joppa."

## Peter's Vision

9 About noon the following day as they were on their journey and approaching the city, Peter went up on the roof to pray. 10 He became hungry and wanted something to eat, and while the meal was being prepared, he fell into a trance. 11 He saw heaven opened and something like a large sheet being let down to earth by its four corners. 12 It contained all kinds of four-footed animals, as well as reptiles and birds. 13 Then a voice told him, "Get up, Peter. Kill

and eat. 14 "Surely not, Lord!" Peter replied. "I have never eaten anything impure or unclean. 15 The voice spoke to him a second time, "Do not call anything impure that God has made clean. 16 This happened three times, and immediately the sheet was taken back to heaven. 17 While Peter was wondering about the meaning of the vision, the men sent by Cornelius found out where Simon's house was and stopped at the gate. 18 They called out, asking if Simon, who was known as Peter, was staying there."

Let's look at Cornelius's story from three contexts.

- The story of Cornelius and Peter in Acts 10:3–18 illustrates that God is not the author of confusion. Prior to this encounter, Peter did not associate with Gentiles; he believed his mission was solely to the Jews and considered Gentiles unclean, refusing to enter their homes. However, as soon as God appeared to Cornelius and instructed him to send for Peter in Joppa, God simultaneously gave Peter a vision that directly addressed his reservations about interacting with what he considered unclean. This coordination highlights God's intentionality and order in unfolding His plans.

- This story shows that, irrespective of your faith, religion, tribe, culture, or creed, God is attracted to kind, moral, humane, good, and honest people with integrity. Cornelius wasn't a Christian when God reached out to him. He was still a Gentile when God located him and went as far as commissioning His angel to connect Cornelius to Peter.

- This story also shows that being good, moral, kind, or actively engaging in community service without Christ is not enough for God. If I may say, doing good and exhibiting good behavior are not peculiar to Christians; even non-Christians who are moralists do the same. The difference is whether you have surrendered your life to Christ in total obedience, and that is what matters to God.

God's heart was drawn to Cornelius as He was touched by his gifts and kindheartedness, but these qualities aren't enough to cement Cornelius' relationship with God. To establish a perfect relationship between God and Cornelius, God had to go through the trouble of linking Cornelius to Peter so he could hear the good news and then accept Christ into his life and household.

One thing particular about God's truth is that it endures and never dies. Every attempt to kill this truth causes it to morph into something bigger, like a snowball getting bigger. This might take the form of a sudden revival movement that overtakes a city and attracts national and global attention.

From the days of Martin Luther OSA, the German priest whose execution gave birth to the Protestant movement, to other more recent outbursts of the Christian faith, we acknowledge that most great revivals happened after major attempts to stifle the Christian faith. Let's look at some major attempts to silence the word of God and what followed in the wake of such attempts:

- Daniel
- The 3 Hebrew children
- The German Martin Luther
- Azusa street revival
- The Welsh revival

Pastor Yomi Olowoyo's book "Divine Ownership" provides insightful explanations and depth on how God used Daniel and the three Hebrew boys (Shadrach, Meshach, and Abednego) to bring about the universal revolution of revival in their days. The fact that these kings' decrees did not come about by accident, but were the result of persecution for which they stood firm in their faith, is an indication that God's truth endures..

Martin Luther, a German theologian, sparked a global religious revival with the Protestant Reformation. His 95 Theses, which critiqued the Catholic Church's practices, particularly the sale of indulgences, served as a catalyst for this movement. The subsequent spread of his ideas, facilitated by the printing press, led to a significant schism in Western Christianity and the emergence of Protestantism.

Luther's actions were driven by a pursuit of sincere devotion to God. What the Church saw as rebellion was not rooted in arrogance; rather, Luther was pointing people toward heaven. He argued that salvation is achieved through faith alone, not through works or indulgences and that the Bible, not the Pope, is the ultimate source of religious authority.

The newly invented printing press allowed Luther's writings to be widely disseminated, spreading his ideas rapidly throughout Europe. His translation of the Bible into German, completed in the 16th century, was a pivotal moment in history. It aimed to make the scriptures accessible to the general public, most of whom did not understand Latin, the language of the Church at the time. When Christ said to preach the good news to everyone, this was that command in action.

Luther was persecuted for his efforts, but this was not in vain. What followed was the emergence of new Protestant denominations, including Lutheranism, Calvinism, and Anglicanism. Efforts to contain the Word of God and the persecutions that followed ultimately resulted in a revival that became the Protestant Reformation. This is how the Christian faith spread and became accessible to all.

The Azusa Street Revival was a historic series of revival meetings that took place in Los Angeles, California. It was led by William

J. Seymour, an African American preacher. The revival began on April 9, 1906, and continued until roughly 1915.

The UK also experienced what we call the Restoration Movement in the 1970s. The movement was led by notable men of God, some of whom include Bryn Jones, Arthur Wallis, Peter Lyne, David Mansell, Graham Perrins, Hugh Thompson, and John Noble. Interestingly, this movement occurred at a time when evangelism was in a sorry state in the UK. These men of God pioneered the Apostolic-Prophetic Movement that focused on restoring the Christian faith to its original glory. For many Christians who seem to think the kind of revivals discussed above are a thing of the past and that the world has moved on from the Christian faith, it would be better to consider a more recent revival like the one that happened at Asbury campus in 2023.

The 2023 Asbury Revival was a Christian revival at Asbury University in Wilmore, Kentucky. Some described this 2023 Asbury

Revival as Gen Z's first revival. The revival was led by students and attracted college students from over 260 colleges and universities. The revival included students reading and reciting scripture, standing with arms raised, praying in small groups, kneeling at the altar, lying prostrate, and talking to each other. The Asbury Revival is not going to be the end of it; we should look forward to seeing many more of this kind of revival in the future. The Christian faith has thrived for over two thousand years because it is God's thing.

Matthew 16:18 "And I say also unto thee, that thou art Peter, and upon this rock I will build My church; and the gates of hell shall not prevail against it".

The church, in this context, represents Christ, and Christ said He is the truth. Therefore, it will be sufficient to rephrase this to mean, "I will announce Myself, and the gates of hell will not prevail against Me." So far, the attempt to keep the word of God out of our lives has largely failed because snowflakes always melt when the sun rises.

In one of my visits to Germany, I remember engaging with a Gypsy lady who claimed to be an atheist. She acknowledged the existence of dark forces but refused to acknowledge the existence of God. I spent some time trying to make her understand that every force has a source, and if there are dark forces in the spirit realm, then they must have a source, which is the devil. She also insisted there is nothing like the forces of light. I was glad for the opportunity to engage in such a conversation, as I made her understand that dark forces have a source, and the fact that we have a force called darkness means the benchmark for determining darkness is light. We eventually ended our conversation as I was able to draw her attention to the fact that if there are forces of darkness, there must also be forces of light, and God is the source of light, while the devil is the source of darkness.

It is obvious that some very outspoken atheists have taken to the airwaves in their push against the Christian faith, and it is important not to let them steal your light. They can be quite convincing in their arguments that there is no God, but when you compare what they say with the alternatives they offer, their arguments immediately fall flat.

Richard Dawkins recently announced himself as a cultural Christian. However, this is far from acknowledging the existence of God and the deity of Christ, but it is a step closer to accepting the moral view of the Christian faith. Cultural Christianity is one thing, but that isn't good enough. Associating with Christian practices and liking Christian values does not necessarily translate into confessing Christ and accepting His Lordship.

Unlike Richard Dawkins, Graham Hancock promotes pseudoscientific ideas about ancient civilizations and hypothetical lost lands and believes in the existence of spirit as per the experience of the Shaman, but he does not believe in God. He believes there is more to man than just living and dying. He believes in the afterlife, but this is about reincarnation. He believes so much in Shamanism that he believes in the Shaman's experience of the spirit realm, yet he struggles to believe in God's existence and the spirit realm that Christ preached about.

Graham Hancock talked about a spiritual experience he once had after taking Ayahuasca, which produces DMT and sent him into that realm where he had an encounter with an intelligent entity, as he called it. After taking Ayahuasca 70 times, he only had this experience once. Yet even from this one unnatural experience, which could be likened to someone hallucinating due to Ayahuasca, he could make nothing out of it.

Graham Hancock believes that there is a hand behind the creation of the universe, and that the beings behind this must have been from a dying planet, which shot bacteria and scattered them

## Light in the Last Days

into the earth. These bacteria somehow evolved into humans. When asked how sure he is about his postulation, Graham said he is not certain. He proceeded to say he is just exploring the possibilities of how the earth came into being.

All these postulations, including the work of Richard Dawkins, start from the middle and ignore how it all started. It is like a man who wants to count from 1 to 10 but starts counting from 5, 6, 7, 8, and so on. Richard Dawkins is undoubtedly a very intelligent man, and his works on biology are a testament to that, but his tireless efforts to disprove the Bible and God flaw his work. Their conversational approach tends to gloss over inconvenient truths, even when those truths are right in front of them. It doesn't matter how it is phrased; a half-truth is not truth, it is something else.

There's no need to fabricate a grand mystery around the idea of a universe existing without God, as if human intelligence without a divine source demands some deeper, hidden explanation.

Thousands of years separate Moses' writing of Genesis from the scientific discovery of the Big Bang, yet the Bible described the origins of the universe with surprising accuracy long before modern science caught up. While science has revealed much, it still cannot account for what came before the Big Bang, a mystery the Bible already touches on. In Genesis, the earth is described as "formless and void" before God spoke. This aligns closely with scientific views that there was essentially nothing prior to the explosion of light and energy.

In Genesis 1:3, God says, "Let there be light," and light bursts into existence not gradually like a sunrise, but as a sudden, dramatic event. There was no concept of morning or night at that point, as day and night were only defined later when God separated the light from the darkness. This account mirrors the sudden nature of the Big Bang more closely than many realize.

Even in Job 38:31, the Bible references Orion's Belt, the "three sisters" stars long before astronomers formally identified it. Scripture holds many such insights, but often, we approach it with the equivalent of a teaspoon when we should be digging with a shovel. If we take the time to truly study and reflect on the Bible, we will uncover truths of immense value, a treasure no one can take from us.

Scientists themselves, including highly regarded scientists like Stephen Hawking and Geoffrey Hinton, have warned that artificial intelligence will, at some point, be able to repair and improve itself. But the truth remains that when that comes, it does not take away the fact that AI started by the hands of humans. The AIs themselves will not begin the kind of arguments we see among atheists, claiming they are a product of coincidence, where some pieces of computer software accidentally collided and suddenly became an intelligent robot.

Unfortunately, the more you examine the basis of some of these anti-God arguments, you find that their arguments lack foundation and merit. All you see are people confusing themselves. When people lose their minds, they lose their senses, because it is a hundred times more convenient to believe that God created the earth than to hope for the possibility that some bacteria were shot into the earth from another planet.

Reading the article Camus' The Plague by Vinoth Ramachandra, let's draw a little insight from the life of the famous atheist Albert Camus, who has influenced the views of many. The context of this conversation isn't about whether Camus died from an accident or suicide but how his view of God changed.

The two quotes below from Vinoth Ramachandra's article relate to Albert Camus in Howard Mumma's book "Albert Camus and the Minister." Howard Mumma brought some illumination into the life and times of Albert Camus:

## *Light in the Last Days*

"Live as a saint [a just man] without God" haunted Camus all his life. And, I was not surprised to learn that, over the course of a few years before his untimely death in 1960, he met regularly with an American Methodist pastor, Howard Mumma, in Paris. Mumma records that Camus read the Bible several times and confessed to him: "The reason I have been coming to church is because I am seeking. I'm almost on a pilgrimage, seeking something to fill the void that I am experiencing, and no one else knows. Certainly, the public and the readers of my novels, while they see that void, are not finding the answers in what they are reading. But deep down, you are right, I am searching for something that the world is not giving me." (Howard Mumma, Albert Camus and the Minister).

Considering the insights from Howard Mumma and the conversations between Albert Camus and the minister, we can conclude that a life without God is an empty one. Albert Camus felt that emptiness and began seeking God to fill that void. Unfortunately, many of his readers were unaware of Albert's secret visits to the priest and his efforts to reconnect with God. Albert Camus' case is not unique. Most atheists are in the same situation, they just haven't made the connection between their emptiness and their godlessness. They see a world filled with troubles, shout about it, and blame God for these issues, but they offer no solutions for the emptiness and the troubles in the world.

I recently watched a conversation between Ayaan Hirsi Ali and Jordan Peterson, as well as a debate between her and Richard Dawkins. Ayaan Hirsi Ali, among other positions, is a senior fellow at the Future of Democracy Project at Harvard Kennedy School.

Ayaan Hirsi Ali was once popular, with her name appearing alongside other famous atheists like Richard Dawkins, Sam Harris, Christopher Hitchens, and Daniel Dennett. Interestingly, she now finds herself debating Richard Dawkins after her personal encounter with God. Much like Albert Camus, who was in the process of reconciling with God before his unfortunate death, Ayaan Hirsi Ali may have led many away from God before her own encounter with Him.

Rosalind Picard, an MIT professor, is another example of an atheist who became agnostic and eventually became a Christian. As a tech pioneer, she was deeply grounded in science and, like many other atheists, believed that everything could be proven through science. Yet, she soon realized that some things intrinsic to human nature, such as love and why we love one person over another, even when both perform the same act of kindness—cannot be proven scientifically.

The bible book of Joel 3:14 "Multitudes, multitudes in the valley of decision! For the day of the LORD is near in the valley of decision."

As you read this, you might be asking yourself, "What if God is real?" I urge you not to gamble your faith further by listening to atheists who may one day turn to God. Today is the best day to make the decision to welcome Christ into your life, for tomorrow may be too late.

As I mentioned earlier about Ayaan Hirsi Ali, Rosalind Picard may have also led many to see the Christian faith as a mere delusion, but she is now in the faith. Unfortunately, some who may have believed her in the past are still caught in the belief that there is no God. There is no time too late to reconcile with God, but as someone who has been there and done that, Rosalind Picard's voice today is making a significant impact, shining a light for many who are still confused about God's existence.

The context of this conversation is not about how many people in the faith they may have discouraged, but rather the fact that they are back in the faith and now preaching the good news. After all, Apostle Paul, who once persecuted Christians, may have caused some to lose their faith before his own encounter with Christ. This, for me, serves as a wake-up call to those in the faith who may one day lose their belief because they listened to the views of an atheist. If you lose your relationship with Christ, you might never have the opportunity to return to the faith, but the atheist who led you away might reconcile with God, even on their deathbed.

Richard Dawkins, for example, argues that we don't know, and he quickly describes God as a mere personification. He is quick to point out all the troubles in the world but offers no solutions to these problems. He promotes the idea of the Big Bang with optimism in his speeches that God does not exist. However, when asked about what preceded the Big Bang, he admits, "We don't know."

Interestingly, many Christians, and people of other faiths who claim to have encountered Christ, testify to the existence of God, yet Dawkins, who admits that he doesn't know, is quick to dismiss these encounters as mere fiction of the mind.

Concepts like truth, beauty, and justice cannot be scientifically proven. These things are subjective from a human perspective. For instance, beauty is said to be in the eye of the beholder, meaning there is no universal definition of beauty because it is intrinsic and beyond science. Similarly, the existence of God cannot be proven through scientific means or empirical deductions. The intrinsic nature of God is such that our inner selves can bear witness to the existence of the divine. The argument of most atheists, including Richard Dawkins, is based on the flawed premise that because they do not understand something, then it does not exist.

Science has proven that we are surrounded by bacteria; our phones, food, desks, and clothing carry bacteria, but we cannot see them. We would have to use a magnifying lens or a microscope to detect them. Similarly, a magnetic field cannot be detected by hand, plastic, or wood, but only by metal. The spiritual realm is the same—we cannot access it without the right tool, and that tool is faith. The fact that some of us are unable to physically operate in that realm does not mean it does not exist. To access the spiritual realm, we need faith, a humble heart, and a seeking spirit. Just as extra effort is required to see bacteria, extra effort is needed to connect with God. Christ said, "If you seek, you will find," which means it is only those who seek who will experience God and feel His presence.

From the natural man's perspective, David killed Goliath because he was so good at what he did, but for a Christian, it was God who used David to kill Goliath. For the natural man, Gideon and his three hundred men defeated the Midianite army because they were so skilled, but for a Christian, it was God who used them to defeat a 135,000-strong Midianite army. Similarly, for the natural man, Elijah must have been on something, or taken some kind of energy drink to outrun a horse, but for a Christian, God gave him the speed.

Many atheists focus on the technological advancements brought about by science and glorify the achievements of scientists, attributing them to human wisdom, while arguing that there is no God. For Christians, however, God uses scientists to discover what He has already placed on earth to help mankind. God will not add to your wisdom the moment you consider yourself wise because you are already too full to accommodate His wisdom.

Today, we have people like Richard Dawkins in the media who go all out to ensure the gospel is never heard. When they eventually talk about Christians, they do so in a derogatory manner. Just like Joseph's brothers tried but failed to extinguish his dream, so too has the world failed in its attempt to extinguish the Christian faith.

The perception of Christians as some kind of creepy crawlies that should be locked away from civilized society is becoming the norm in many Western societies. As the saying goes, "A lie can travel halfway around the world while the truth is still putting on its shoes." This reflects the media's attempt to silence the narrative of God. Unfortunately, what we face today is nothing compared to the persecution Christians faced in the past. Cutting off a man's tongue to stop him from speaking does not necessarily mean he is wrong, it's simply a fear of what he has to say.

The Bible reveals that the Philistines strategically targeted blacksmiths in Israel, a calculated move to cripple the Israelites' ability to produce weapons and defend themselves. At first, it might have seemed insignificant; after all, only the blacksmiths were being attacked. But over time, the Israelites would come to realize that their defense had been silently weakened without blacksmiths, their ability to wage war was gone.

In the same way, blacksmiths were essential to a nation's strength and preparedness, so too is the Christian faith vital to the moral and spiritual stability of our world. Today, many who attack the Christian faith don't realize they are unknowingly being used by the enemy to achieve a deeper and darker agenda. Jesus called us the salt of the earth and the light of the world (see Matthew 5:13–14). This means that the Christian faith is the primary force resisting the spread of spiritual darkness.

Romans 14:17 tell us "the kingdom of God is not a matter of eating and drinking, but of righteousness, peace, and joy in the Holy Spirit." These are things the devil cannot truly offer. You may find fleeting joy in the world, but not lasting joy. And as for peace, the kind that settles the soul, only Christ can give that. The world simply cannot.

Today's media is caught up in the illusion of a world that can be made beautiful without God's intervention. Life can often be filled with misery, broken hearts, unfulfilled dreams, and all we have left is hope. This hope is significant because it signifies a ray of light, a belief that what we hope for will come true and our fears will not materialize. With God, every day is like spring, representing hope, new beginnings, and second chances in the midst of harsh conditions. Sometimes, we find ourselves in a "dog house" with God because of our unfulfilled expectations.

Humans are part spirit, and our God is a spirit. Only those who activate their spiritual being will be able to access God, who is fully a spirit being. On rare occasions, God reveals Himself to people who are not spiritual, whether because He has plans for them or simply because He wants to reveal Himself to them.

Many today are in the middle, more agnostic than atheist, because they do not see physical proof of God in heaven controlling the affairs of men. If we look at the world through the eyes of an agnostic, it would be easy to conclude that there is no God, especially if God Himself did not come to rescue their unbelief.

There are several instances in the Bible where God seems silent or absent, and people live as though there is no God. The Israelites' slavery in Egypt lasted for hundreds of years, during which they were enslaved, helpless, and hopeless. Though they were aware of their God, they felt He had forsaken them. The Egyptians, too, dismissed the story of the Israelites' God as a myth. However, God eventually showed up, and Pharaoh and his people experienced the God of heaven.

The story of the three Hebrew children is another example. When King Nebuchadnezzar invaded Israel and plundered the nation, God did not intervene to stop the invasion. As far as the Babylonians were concerned, the story of the God of Israel was a myth. But when the three Hebrew children refused to bow to the golden image and were thrown into the fiery furnace, God, the God they thought didn't exist, showed up. I must confess to you that the idea that humans can do without God is nothing short of craziness on steroids. Craziness by itself is already crazy enough, but when crazy is on steroids, it becomes foolishness on a whole new level..

Daniel 3:23-27 [NIV]. "23 And these three men, Shadrach, Meshach, and Abednego, fell down bound into the midst of the burning fiery furnace.

24 Then Nebuchadnezzar the king was astonished, and rose up in haste, and spake, and said unto his counsellors, Did not we cast three men bound into the midst of the fire? They answered and said unto the king, True, O king.

25 He answered and said, Lo, I see four men loose, walking in the midst of the fire, and they have no hurt; and the form of the fourth is like the Son of God.

26 Then Nebuchadnezzar came near to the mouth of the burning fiery furnace, and spake, and said, Shadrach, Meshach, and Abednego, ye servants of the most high God, come forth, and come hither. Then Shadrach, Meshach, and Abednego, came forth of the midst of the fire.

27 And the princes, governors, and captains, and the king's counsellors, being gathered together, saw these men, upon whose bodies the fire had no power, nor was an hair of their head singed, neither were their coats changed, nor the smell of fire had passed on them.

28 Then Nebuchadnezzar spake, and said, Blessed be the God of Shadrach, Meshach, and Abednego, who hath sent his angel, and delivered his servants that trusted in him, and have changed the king's word, and yielded their bodies, that they might not serve nor worship any god, except their own God."

Nebuchadnezzar eventually realised the God of heaven is real and it did not take much for the king to submit to the God of heaven.

The next story is found in Daniel 5:1-31, regarding Belshazzar, the king of Babylon, who used golden and silver cups taken from the temple in Jerusalem when his father, King Nebuchadnezzar, invaded Israel.

The interesting thing about this story is that God was silent when King Nebuchadnezzar invaded Jerusalem, killed thousands or tens of thousands of Israelites, took many captives, looted the temple, and possibly killed some priests in the process. God did not act when they took the gold and silver cups, and He did not act for years while these cups were in the custody of Nebuchadnezzar. It was as if the God of the Israelites did not exist, and it seemed as though the whole story about this God was some kind of hype. However, on this particular day, the God of heaven, invisible to the eyes, made His finger visible.

God did not just smite Belshazzar with some quiet sickness. He showed Belshazzar and his cohorts that He exists before bringing Belshazzar's throne to an immediate end.

There are several stories across the Bible similar to the one above, where God seems silent but eventually shows up after a long while. This is what it looks like in our world today, and it has led many people to consider the Bible merely an anecdotal manual. The truth remains that God's silence doesn't necessarily mean He is absent. His absence is not implied by perceived silence; He is still there, even if we can't readily feel or hear His presence.

God has been around long before all these self-proclaimed atheists were born. He is therefore accustomed to people with atheist views. Consider the Israelites, who, despite witnessing God's miracles and mercy firsthand, still rebelled against God, to their own peril, unfortunately.

If we don't need God to decide what is morally right, our morality becomes relative without Him. No individual or nation can live out their moral view. It is obvious that no individual can be consistent with their moral values at all times and in all circumstances. Take a nation like the United States, for instance; you will realize that the United States treats different nations differently, even when the circumstances are the same.

For example, if we think our view on morality is right and our next-door neighbor thinks his or her view on morality is equally right, who then is right, and who is wrong? Most societies and cultures around the world have different views when it comes to cultural values and morality. This brings to the forefront the question of which nation's moral values are right, and which are wrong?

Consequently, it is impossible for any individual to live out their morality consistently. In other words, human beings cannot live morally at all times, irrespective of the circumstances, unless there is a set standard with which we can measure our morality.

Some have argued that in a world with rational human beings, there is no need for God's moral compass to guide the affairs of men. However, people can be rational and still not be able to differentiate between good and evil, based on how their conscience is set. Some of the world's worst conspiracies and most evil acts committed by men are carried out by rational minds that chose to use their rationality to do unspeakable evil.

God's moral compass should serve as a benchmark for us to know when we are morally below standard. Therefore, if a man who cannot consistently live out his morality becomes a judge of his own self, then the world will be taken over by partial decisions that lack objectivity. In the same way, no nation can live out its moral view without being guided by the moral compass of a Divine rule giver who sets moral standards that cut across societies and cultures.

On the other hand, God has been consistent with His moral values. He loved the Israelites so much and delivered them from Pharaoh. But for the very first time, the same God allowed 23,000 of His beloved Israelites, who never lost more than thirty-six men in war, to fall into the hands of the Moabites because of sexual immorality . (1 Corinthians 10: 8-9, We should not commit sexual immorality, as some of them did-and in one day twenty-three thousand of them died. We should not test Christ as some of them did-and were killed by snakes).

God also allowed the Israelites to fall into the hands of the men of Ai because there were stolen items buried in the camp of the Israelites by Achan (Joshua 7:1-28). God even turned His back on His Son, Jesus Christ, the moment the sins of the whole world were placed on Him. In like manner, Jesus Christ taught us to love our enemies and pray for those who persecute us.

(Mathew 5:43-44; You have heard that it was said, 'Love your neighbour and hate your enemy.' But I say unto you, Love your enemies, bless them that curse you, do good to them that hate you, and pray for them which despitefully use you and persecute you) . Christ on His part, live out His teachings whilst on the cross (Luke 23:34; Jesus said, "Father, forgive them, for they do not know what they are doing." And they divided up his clothes by casting lots).

Jesus Christ's actions were consistent with His teachings. He taught us to pray for those who persecute us, and even on the cross, He actually put His words into action by praying for those who persecuted Him, asking His Father to forgive those who persecuted Him, for they knew not what they did. This means that God has been consistent with His view on morality, irrespective of the circumstances, and He won't change that with you or with me.

Christ offered forgiveness to Saul even when Saul was persecuting Him (Acts 9:4-7 [NIV]: "4 He fell to the ground and heard a voice say to him, "Saul, Saul, why do you persecute me?" 5 "Who are you, Lord?" Saul asked. "I am Jesus, whom you are persecuting," he replied. 6 "Now get up and go into the city, and you will be told what you must do." 7 The men traveling with Saul stood there speechless; they heard the sound but did not see anyone."

Saul encountered Christ at a time when he was determined to kill and imprison Christians. Saul did not get the just deserts he deserved, as many had expected. He was not struck dead in return for the death he'd wished upon God's people. Christ forgave Saul and gave him a second chance, something many of Christ's disciples at the time might have considered as God being overly lenient. Even the disciples were kind of wary of having Saul in their midst because they knew what he was capable of before his road to Damascus encounter. The disciples knew of the forgiveness Christ preached; they even preached it, but it was a bit hard to stomach when Christ extended that forgiveness to Saul.

It is now pertinent to state that relative morality has crept into the church, and this has greatly impacted the Church's ability to exert influence and confront the decay in our society. There is no difference between most Christians and others out there who do not believe in God.

Presently, in some churches, the congregation wants the pastors and priests to preach what they want to hear and not the mind of God. It's so sad that some pastors have fallen prey to this deadly poison, and this has brought so much decay to the body of Christ. If, as Christians, we don't want God's ministers to speak about God's standard on morality, we are no different from the man in the street who says there is no God or that he doesn't need a God to tell him what's right or wrong.

Because now, you are deciding what message you want to hear and how you want the message to be preached.

This shift from the truth could be the result of the priests or pastors caving in to pressure from lukewarm members, or the priests, on their own initiative, wanting to water down the word of God just to go along with secular trends.

Moral values may vary from one nation or culture to another, but Christian values remain the same, irrespective of culture or nation. Therefore, being in the United Kingdom, the United States, Nigeria, China or anywhere in the world does not mean God's position on morality is suddenly relegated to the bin. God's view on morality has been relevant from age to age, generation to generation. The questioning of the relevance of the Bible in our lives today, resulting from the argument that our civilization is quite different from the time of Moses and Jesus Christ—means those who read the word of God for the sake of criticism won't find the light it shines.

Moreover, God only answers to those who seek Him in truth and faith. We might not find God and won't hear from Him if we think too little of Him.

Proverbs 9:10-12 (NKJV) "The fear of the LORD is the beginning of wisdom, And the knowledge of the Holy One is understanding. For by me your days will be multiplied, And years of life will be added to you."

Therefore, it is only God's moral values, which cut across nations, cultures, and tribes, that can serve as a moral benchmark for humanity. This will help mankind hold nations and individuals accountable when their actions fall below standard.

# CHAPTER THREE

*When our Journey here on earth ends*

Many who have returned from near-death experiences have spoken about how their whole life flashed before their eyes, like a movie. Those who witnessed family members pass away often say that the last few minutes didn't resemble someone on the verge of decomposing into manure, but rather someone letting go of their mortal body and heading somewhere. That "somewhere" is the unknown, which forms the subject of this discourse.

The problem of the world we live in today, be it morality, ethics, scientific or whatever, all boils down to philosophical perceptions of humans. Some people prefer to abide by the law, while others choose to break it. Some are oppressed, while others are oppressors. Some are conservative, while others are progressive. Some are capitalists, while others are socialists or even communists. All these differing views and philosophical standpoints are often in conflict, making the world a difficult place to live in, with some seeking peace, while others seek justice..

In a world filled with suffering, wrongdoing, and unpunished evil, the question of justice becomes a deeply personal and philosophical concern. Every day, stories surface of innocent individuals languishing in prisons for crimes they did not commit, while those truly responsible walk freely among us. Families mourn lost loved ones taken by violence, while the perpetrators evade consequences. History is full of individuals who inflicted tremendous pain and yet lived long, seemingly blessed lives, untouched by the weight of their actions. In such a reality, where is justice to be found?

The human justice system, as noble as its intentions may be, is riddled with flaws. Errors in investigation, bias, corruption, and systemic inequalities often lead to wrongful convictions or the failure to convict at all. For many, the idea of karma, an unseen moral force that balances scales over time offers some hope. However, it is clear that karma does not always deliver its verdicts within a person's lifetime. There are far too many examples of people who lived unjustly and yet escaped any observable form of retribution.

This reality raises a profound question: if there is no God, how are these injustices ultimately addressed? Without a higher power, without an all-knowing, all-seeing judge, then some of the worst atrocities may never face any reckoning. Is that a world we can accept?

This is where the concept of God and more specifically, the idea of divine judgment enters with significance. The belief in a just God who sees all, who knows the heart and intentions behind every action, offers a necessary moral framework. It introduces the idea that life does not end with death, and that beyond the grave, every soul will stand accountable for the choices they made on earth. In this view, life after death is not just a comforting thought, it is a cornerstone of justice.

The promise of divine judgment assures that no deed, whether good or evil, goes unnoticed. It means that every injustice that slipped through the cracks of human courts will one day be brought to light and addressed with perfect fairness. It gives meaning to the struggle of those who suffer unjustly and encourages righteousness even when it appears unrewarded.

*Light in the Last Days*

In a world where justice is often delayed, distorted, or denied, the existence of God and the hope of divine judgment provide the moral anchor that sustains the cry for true justice. Without that, we are left with a void, where some wrongs may never be righted, and the weight of injustice may remain forever unresolved.

Governments around the world have continued their efforts to address issues relating to crime and injustice by introducing laws. When these laws fail to resolve the issues at hand, new laws are introduced, and more are added, yet these injustices persist. Despite the hundreds and thousands of years since the Bible was written, humanity has still not come up with ideas that rival the Bible's propositions for addressing these issues.

God might not go as far as physically wagging His fingers in the sky for humans to see to prove His existence. He has tried it before when He spoke directly to the Israelites (millions of them), it didn't work. Interestingly, after many mind-boggling miracles performed right before their eyes, they still requested that God speak to them directly, and He did. They heard His voice, yet many of them still did not place their faith in Him.

The question remains: if those who witnessed miracles and even heard God speak still forgot Him and went about doing their own thing, why would God want to further prove His existence to humans?

As it stands, God has left humanity with the choice of either believing in Him through faith, even when we haven't seen Him, or doing our own thing. There are many people who have a curious fixation on seeing something out of the ordinary before they can believe in God. The thing about the Christian faith is that you believe to see, not the other way around.

In the week preceding the COVID-19 lockdown in the UK, the news of deaths dominated the airwaves, and the silent echoes and whispers of death were what many could hear. I remember during the Sunday service just a day before the lockdown, Pastor Tunde Alabi was preaching and suddenly focused on Acts 27:23-44 as led by the Holy Spirit. He then declared to the church members, saying that just as God assured Paul, "no member of the church will be lost to the pandemic." Interestingly, while there was news of deaths all around us, no member of Christian Life Centre was lost to COVID-19. The pastor's pronouncement might seem insignificant, but because we believed, it came to pass.

The miracle of turning water into wine happened only in the act of doing. The Assyrian general was healed of his leprosy while believing and carrying out the instructions of Elisha. The two loaves and five fish only multiplied as they broke the bread and shared it. The little jar of oil continued to pour out as long as there were jars available to fill.

## Light in the Last Days

God is keen on simple obedience and would hardly use overly dramatic means to speak to people. Let's consider the days of Noah, God did not show any sign in the clouds to prove to the people that the rain was coming. All God used was the voice of Noah, a voice just like that of any preacher on your street, nothing out of the ordinary.

Another story is that of Jonah and the people of Nineveh. God did not use some overly dramatic means to warn the people of Nineveh, just the voice of Jonah, like the voice of any preacher on your street.

We can see that God was very involved in Jonah's assignment from the start. From when God gave him the instruction, to his escape to Tarshish, his time in the belly of the whale, and his eventual transportation to the shores of Nineveh, yet God did not do anything out of the ordinary to warn the people of Nineveh, just the voice of Jonah, a man walking the streets and asking the people to repent. This is no different from the voice you hear on your streets asking you to turn to God. Have you stopped to ponder the trouble God went through to get that preacher on the street at that particular point in time, just for you to hear his or her voice?

Looking at the outcomes of Noah's and Jonah's messages: the people in Noah's time did not listen and were destroyed, but the people of Nineveh turned to God and were preserved. All that matters to God is your reaction when you hear "God said." God values simple obedience. What did you do when you heard, "God said?" Unfortunately, there are now people who claim to speak on behalf of God, saying "God said," when in reality, He never did. As a result, discernment is essential, and confirmation becomes important. However, the message of repentance is always relevant, there's no need for confirmation to recognize the need to change your ways when you hear a call to repent.

We can even go a step further and conclude that the people of Nineveh were like good soil because they heard the word and turned a new leaf. God is omniscient, which explains why God disagreed with Jonah on how to approach the people of Nineveh.

Jonah saw bad people who did not deserve God's mercy, but God saw good soil, a people who would be at their best behavior once God showed them the way. A people who would be quicker to turn a new leaf at God's warning than even the Jewish people themselves. This also serves as a lesson for Christian brethren not to be quick to write people off. Judgment is up to God; ours is to continue trusting God for people's repentance.

The king of Nineveh repented and issued a public proclamation that called for the people of Nineveh to fast, wear sackcloth, pray to God, and turn away from evil and violence. The manner in which the king himself took off his robe, put on sackcloth, and sat in ashes was a testament to a people who will do right if they know better. God saw the people's repentance and changed His mind, deciding not to destroy the city.

All they heard was Jonah's voice, nothing out of the ordinary and they repented. Please note that God might be making an effort to reach you through this message, or through the one you heard in the street or in your church the other day. It took God a lot of effort to reach the people of Nineveh, and He is making the same effort to reach you.

Many have argued and described God as harsh over His decision to limit eternal life only to those who believe in Him. But God's position is that if a man chooses not to have anything to do with God while on earth, God, in turn, will not want anything to do with that man after their journey on earth ends.

If I may use this phrase, many of us "social Christians," who adjust our Christian faith to accommodate controversial worldviews, just to be seen as politically correct, to avoid backlash, and to be loved by all, should understand that our race here on earth will come to an end one day. Then, we will be left with nothing to show to our Maker except the fact that we compromised and associated with the world when we had the opportunity to choose God.

I once asked my son if he remembers anything about himself before he was born, anything at all, and he said he remembers nothing. I asked my other son the same question, and he also said he remembers nothing. God is in charge of your pre-life—whatever manner you existed before you were born. He is also in charge of your life on earth and even in charge of your afterlife. This reflects God's complete sovereignty over an individual's existence.

Jeremiah 1:5 God said He knew you before you were formed in your mother's womb, which explains God's attention to details. Interestingly, God knows you before you are born because you already existed as a soul in the spirit realm. Once your journey on earth ends, you will still return to that spirit realm where God reigns supreme.

An average Muslim knows about Christ. They might not have a revelation of Him as God or the Son of God, but they certainly know Him as a prophet. This indicates that Christ has been revealed to the people of the Middle East. God's intention is that every nation, man, and woman on earth hears the message of Christ. The Western nations have heard that message, and now it is an opportunity for those in Asian nations. We in the West have heard the good news (the message of Christ), but the choice is ours: whether to continue embracing it or decide to reject it. The next step will be judgment, based on the fact that we are no longer ignorant of the message of Christ.

God answers the prayers of both Christians and non-Christians. Your religious background does not prevent God from responding to your prayers, except when those prayers are considered detestable to Him (see Matthew 5:45).

What sets a relationship with Christ apart is that it establishes a covenant with God, one that grants us the promise of eternal life in heaven and empowers us to gain deeper insight and direction during our time on earth.

Think of it like visiting a law firm: anyone can walk in and be treated with kindness. You may sit on a comfortable sofa, enjoy the air conditioning, and even have a drink of water. But unless you've signed a contract, the lawyers aren't obligated to represent you in court. In the same way, while God's general kindness is extended to all, only those in covenant with Him through Christ receive the full benefits of that relationship.

I have many friends who belong to other faiths, many of them Atheists, Muslims, Hindus, and so on. My love for them does not wane because of their religious beliefs. We still share gifts and exchange views, but these relationships are limited to our earthly pilgrimage. My desire for them is that we all make it to heaven based on the salvation Christ provides.

Whether you are rich or a pauper, when you die, you will be buried, leaving everything behind. Whether you are a professor, a PhD holder, or a primary school certificate holder, when you die, you will leave those titles behind. Whether you have many children or none at all (whether impotent or barren), when you die, you will leave all your children behind.

Whether you are strong, large in size, or small and tiny, when you die, you will leave your body behind. Whether you are beautiful or ugly, when you die, you will leave your looks behind. Whether you are intelligent or a dullard, when you die, you will leave your memory behind. Whether you are a man or a woman, when you die, you will leave your gender behind.

All the above represents the nothingness of human life. The only thing that will matter after the drama of our earthly journey is the crown God gives to us when we come before Him to account for our time here on earth.

# CHAPTER FOUR

*The Mystery of how God works*

Let's meditate on these few Bible verses, as they will bring some illumination into the mystery of how God works. The God-Christ relationship is at the center of this mystery, because to understand God, we must understand Christ.

John 10:30 Christ said, "I and my father are one." John 5:19 [NIV]. 19 Jesus gave them this answer: "Very truly I tell you, the Son can do nothing by himself; he can do only what he sees his Father doing, because whatever the Father does the Son also does.

"John 14:7-10 [NIV]. 7 "If you really know me, you will know[a] my Father as well. From now on, you do know him and have seen him." 8 Philip said, "Lord, show us the Father and that will be enough for us." 9 Jesus answered: "Don't you know me, Philip, even after I have been among you such a long time? Anyone who has seen me has seen the Father. How can you say, 'Show us the Father'? 10 Don't you believe that I am in the Father, and that the Father is in me? The words I say to you I do not speak on my own authority."

The mystery of how God works will always leave the natural human mind confused. This is because God is the Father and, at the same time, He is the Son. He is a Lion and, at the same time, a Lamb. He has a legion of angels at His beck and call, yet He remained silent and didn't open His mouth as He was led like a Lamb to the slaughter.

You need to die to yourself to overcome spiritual death, just as Christ had to die to overcome death. By His stripes, we are healed; His wounds and pain healed our pain. Moses needed to lift a bronze snake to overcome the snake bite.

To conquer death, we had to experience it in some form. Dying with Christ is a transformative event that triumphs over spiritual death. While the idea of using death to defeat death may seem illogical to some, history shows that similar principles apply in medicine. For instance, elements of a disease are often used to combat that same disease. Snake venom is used to treat snake bites, and even the COVID-19 vaccine was derived from the virus itself. In the wilderness, Moses lifted a bronze snake to heal those bitten, as no antidote was available.

Likewise, overcoming death requires undergoing spiritual death, dying with Christ and putting to death the desires of the flesh, which symbolize our old nature. Only through this process can we rise again with Christ.

If we consider the snake bite attack on the children of Israel while in the wilderness, we will discover that God asked Moses to build a bronze snake and requested that anyone who looks up to the bronze snake on the cross (which represents Christ) will be healed. The thing is, looking at the bronze serpent was such a simple task, yet a good number of the Israelites did not look at this bronze serpent and they died because of it.

We can look at the symbolism of this from two different perspectives.

Firstly, a focus on our problems will not bring the solution we seek; rather, our focus on Christ, as represented by the bronze serpent, will bring the solution we need.

## *Light in the Last Days*

The bible said the thief comes only to steal and kill and destroy; I have come that they may have life, and have it to the full. Christ's life giving grace was demonstrated through our focus on the bronze snake that represents Christ on the cross.

In like manner, considering Matthew 14:25-32 [NIV]. Let's look at what transpired between Christ and Peter.

25 Shortly before dawn Jesus went out to them, walking on the lake. 26 When the disciples saw him walking on the lake, they were terrified. "It's a ghost," they said, and cried out in fear. 27 But Jesus immediately said to them: "Take courage! It is I. Don't be afraid." 28 "Lord, if it's you," Peter replied, "tell me to come to you on the water."

29 "Come," he said. Then Peter got down out of the boat, walked on the water and came toward Jesus. 30 But when he saw the wind, he was afraid and, beginning to sink, cried out, "Lord, save me!" 31 Immediately Jesus reached out his hand and caught him. "You of little faith," he said, "why did you doubt?" 32 And when they climbed into the boat, the wind died down."

Peter sank because he took his eyes off Jesus and focused on the problems around him, which overwhelmed him. Someone once said, "Don't tell God how big your problems are, tell your problems how big your God is." Matthew 9:29 said, "Let it be done for you according to your faith."

Arguably, those who died of snake bites in the wilderness wanted healing but did not want to get their healing God's way. Merely lifting their heads to look at the bronze snake cost these Israelites nothing, but the stubbornness of their hearts led them to prefer death over obedience to God. And God, in His part, was reinforcing His position, that it must be His way, by allowing some of these Israelites to die.

God is keen on our obedience; He will always ask something of us, no matter how simple the task is, just to test our obedience.

God understands the nature of the human heart and knows full well that the devil is keen on shifting man's attention away from God.

The conversation between God and Satan in the Bible book of Job brings further illumination of God's test of our obedience.

Job 1:8-12 [NIV]. "8 Then the Lord said to Satan, "Have you considered my servant Job? There is no one on earth like him; he is blameless and upright, a man who fears God and shuns evil."

9 "Does Job fear God for nothing?" Satan replied. 10 "Have you not put a hedge around him and his household and everything he has? You have blessed the work of his hands, so that his flocks and herds are spread throughout the land. 11 But now stretch out your hand and strike everything he has, and he will surely curse you to your face."

12 The Lord said to Satan, "Very well, then, everything he has is in your power, but on the man himself do not lay a finger."

From the above conversation, we can see that God is not responsible for the troubles of humans, but the devil is. It is important to state that God was the one who pointed Satan to Job, a situation no sane person would want to find themselves in. Sometimes, we might not know why God gives us certain instructions or why He permits certain situations in our lives. With time, we might understand or may never know why God allowed certain situations in our lives.

Job had a good and peaceful life, with everything going well for him. Anyone enjoying something that resembles a normal life, like what Job had, would not want God to point them to a tormentor who would strip them of all they have. God was doing what any proud father would normally do, proudly showing off a child that you are proud of. God's pride in Job relates more to Job's obedience than his wealth.

Unfortunately, this boast by God resulted in Satan making a request to test Job. God is all-knowing, and we cannot say He had no knowledge that this innocent conversation with Satan would

*Light in the Last Days*

take a fatal twist. God, on His part, wanted to prove to Satan that Job is obedient to the last and that there is nothing too spoiled that He cannot restore. God also used this test to prove to Satan that He stands by those who put their faith in Him. In this case, God did, resulting in Job losing everything and eventually being restored by God.

Arguably, many who blame God for their troubles can now see that God is not our tormentor. However, God sometimes allows Satan to torment us to either test our obedience or bring us onto the right path. Considering obedience as the key to our walk with God, we will now consider how this plays a role in God's approach to making things happen.

# CHAPTER FIVE

## *The God, Man Approached*

God's approach to making things happen in the affairs of men is one of partnership and willing participation. God can do things by Himself, but He makes it His style to involve humans.

God can name the animals by Himself, but He asked Adam to do this. God was able to chase the Assyrian army from their camp by Himself, but He chose to use four hungry lepers to do this. The God who can bring down the walls of Jericho still wanted the Israelites to play a part in the process.

The God who can, by Himself, make the three armies fight each other and destroy themselves (2 Chronicles 20) would rather have the Israelites do this with Him by asking them to show up at the battle field.

If you ask for anything, He will usually say yes. The only condition is whether you have what it takes to receive what you've requested. The God of the Bible is able and has the final say in all matters, but He gives us the free will to choose whether or not to agree with Him. God is all-sufficient but loves partnership as much as spending time with humans. He comes down in the cool of the evening to hang out with Adam and Eve.

*Light in the Last Days*

The idea of God as a malevolent father seeking an opportunity to punish us is simply not true.

The attitude of the elder brother in the story of the prodigal son was that of a slave. He talked only about how hard he worked for his dad, but he forgot that everything was his. All he focused on was how hard he worked for his father and received nothing. His frustration was expressed as if he saw his father as a user who makes others labor for him without receiving anything in return. Interestingly, his younger brother seemed to have a better understanding of his relationship with his father. This was because he saw himself as a son and knew that, as a son, he was entitled to an inheritance.

Luke 15:17 says, "When the younger brother came to his senses, he said to himself that even his father's slaves are well-fed," which indicates his understanding of the difference between a son and a slave. More so, when he requested that his father's property be shared between himself and his brother, he didn't include his father's slaves in the sharing formula. Even though inheritances are typically shared only when the owner of the property is deceased, he requested his share while his father was still alive, and he was kind of certain that his request would be granted. This is because he perceived his father as benevolent. On the other hand, the elder brother, who was first in line for inheritance, perceived their father as malevolent, thinking that if he asked, he would not receive.

Unfortunately, this is where many of us miss it—our picture of God determines our relationship with Him, and it shapes how we relate to Him. The father's response in verse 31 reveals the heart of God to us.

Luke 15:31 [NIV]: "'My son,' the father said, 'you are always with me, and everything I have is yours.'"

The story of these two brothers also has implications for self-righteous Christians who judge their relationship with Christ based on their behavior and living by the law, Christians who pride themselves on their moral living rather than on grace. Living right is good in itself, but the truth is that we might live right and still have hearts that aren't right.

It was so obvious that the elder brother was focused on the sin of his brother and did a good job of accusing the younger brother before their father. Many Christians who have fallen are finding it hard to return to church because of how they might be treated by self-righteous Christians who spend most of their time blaming others.

Let's consider the Parable of the Pharisee and the Tax Collector. Luke 18:9-14 [NIV]. 9 To some who were confident of their own righteousness and looked down on everyone else, Jesus told this parable: 10 "Two men went up to the temple to pray, one a Pharisee and the other a tax collector. 11 The Pharisee stood by himself and prayed: 'God, I thank you that I am not like other people—robbers, evildoers, adulterers—or even like this tax collector. 12 I fast twice a week and give a tenth of all I get.'

13 "But the tax collector stood at a distance. He would not even look up to heaven, but beat his breast and said, 'God, have mercy on me, a sinner.'

14 "I tell you that this man, rather than the other, went home justified before God. For all those who exalt themselves will be humbled, and those who humble themselves will be exalted."

My wife, Nkem, once said that the prodigal son is more like the tax collector in the story above, while his elder brother's actions were not in any way different from that of the Pharisee.

From Christ's comment above, we can safely conclude that it is easier to gain heaven's attention by raising our hands in surrender and saying, "Lord, I am unworthy; please have mercy on me and accept me," than by justifying our adherence to the law.

The father in the story of the Prodigal Son showed a desire to have his son come into the house and join the party. He enjoyed having his sons around. The Bible says that God comes down in the cool of the evening to fellowship with Adam and Eve. They were not guessing His presence; they felt His presence in the garden because they could hear His footsteps.

With the Israelites, He would have loved to hang out with them, but because of their sinful nature, He preferred that an angel go with them. Moses, however, preferred God's presence to being accompanied by angels. He knew that the presence of God is everything. God's nature of holiness meant that He could not behold sin, and this implied that His being in their midst would pose a great risk for the Israelites. God knew this beforehand, which is why He told Moses in Exodus 32:10 [NIV], "Now leave me alone so that my anger may burn against them and that I may destroy them. Then I will make you into a great nation." It was not God's initial intention to not go with the Israelites, but His nature of not being able to behold sin would put the people at risk.

God eventually went with them following Moses' plea, and the people could see the cloud during the day and the pillar of fire at night. They never guessed if that was Him, they knew it was God.

God enjoys the company of men and looks for every opportunity to hang out with us, but this is only possible if we are able to create the right environment for Him to stay, which is a life free from sin. The God-man partnership only works if we create the right atmosphere that allows God to dwell with us.

God spent some time in a back-and-forth conversation with Jonah as he sat down at a place east of the city of Nineveh, as stated in the Bible in Jonah 4:2-11.

There had been several heart-to-heart conversations between God and Jonah preceding verses 9 to 11, but their exchange in verses 9 to 11 shows the heart of God—the kind of conversation we see between a father and a son.

9 But God said to Jonah, "Is it right for you to be angry about the plant?"

"It is," he said. "And I'm so angry I wish I were dead."

10 But the Lord said, "You have been concerned about this plant, though you did not tend it or make it grow. It sprang up overnight and died overnight.

11 And should I not have concern for the great city of Nineveh, in which there are more than a hundred and twenty thousand people who cannot tell their right hand from their left—and also many animals?"

Christ is a true reflection of God's nature, and just like God, we can see these similarities in Christ's dealings with people. Christ wanted to spend more time with the people and, instead of sending them away because it was getting dark and they lacked food, He intervened with a miracle. He used every opportunity to engage and make God's nature clearer.

He hung out with the prostitutes, visited Zacchaeus' house, chatted with the Samaritan woman by the well, regularly visited Mary and Martha's home, and the list goes on.

In all the cases mentioned above, the people had a better grasp of God and were reconciled with Him. Even though Christ had foreknowledge about the lifestyles of these people, He wasn't too quick to point that out. Instead, He chose to hang out with them so that they would know Him better, thereby knowing God better.

Sometimes, our expectations become distorted and often clash with God's plan for our lives. But in His infinite mercy, God doesn't allow us to walk blindly into trouble, He steps in and redirects our path, even if it means forcing a change.

I have a relative who, during the Nigerian Civil War, was presented with what seemed like a once-in-a-lifetime opportunity. He was in his late twenties at the time, and had been asked to accompany his elder sister's husband on a critical mission, delivering salaries to Biafran soldiers and others in their service. His brother-in-law was a well-known businessman, even before the war broke out, and the assignment was not only patriotic but also highly lucrative due to the risks involved.

It was the kind of opportunity that could have changed his life, and he already saw himself stepping into wealth. But his plans took an unexpected turn when his mother strongly objected, fearing the dangers of encountering Nigerian soldiers along the way. Disheartened by her refusal, he turned to his eldest brother, his mother's first son, hoping for support. But his brother agreed with their mother and advised him against going.

Feeling betrayed by his family, he approached his favorite uncle, especially since his father had passed away. This uncle had always backed him in the past, but to his surprise, even he took the side of his mother and brother.

Left with no choice, he stayed back while his brother-in-law proceeded alone. Tragically, along the way, his brother-in-law was captured by Nigerian soldiers. He was forced to dig his own grave, climb into it, and was executed and buried in the very grave he had dug.

This story may not mirror your exact situation, but I want you to consider that it could be God standing in your way, just as He did with Balaam, or with the young man in the story above. That young man was already an adult, fully capable of making his own decisions, and he knew it. Yet, he allowed God to use his mother, elder brother, and uncle to intervene, and ultimately, to save his life.

So I ask you, what are you thinking right now, and who might God be using to speak to you? Is there someone you've dismissed, thinking they have no right to advise you, just because you believe you're old enough to decide for yourself?

This young man came to understand what God had saved him from in just a few weeks. For some of us, it may take years to fully grasp what God has done in our lives. And in other cases, we may never fully know. But what matters most is this, trust that God has your back. When things aren't going your way, remember, God is not finished with you yet.

God is not a father who is actively looking for faults and seeking an opportunity to punish you. Just like our earthly fathers are actively guiding us and correcting our wrongs, so is God.

After Abraham and his wife, Sarah, concocted the idea of having a child through Hagar, which resulted in the dilemma of Ishmael, God came to Abraham in the Bible book of Genesis 21:8–21. This time, God did not dwell on the Ishmael situation. Rather, He gave Abraham a directive on the way forward. God opened a new chapter by reintroducing Himself to Abraham and restating a fresh relationship with him. God, however, asked Abraham to walk in perfection this time.

When Peter denied Christ and fell short, Christ corrected Peter's wrong and still made him lead the disciples. During one of His final appearances, He asked Peter to feed His flock (John 21:15-17). Hence, Peter remained the foundation of the church. Christ did not leave Thomas to wallow in confusion and doubt. Instead, He came back to address Thomas's doubt so that Thomas's fresh start after the resurrection would be perfect.

This is what the God-man approach is about, it is not about a father seeking out an opportunity to punish. Rather, it is about a father keen on directing our path.

When Abraham pleaded with God to spare his nephew, Lot, God did not say that it was not His concern; rather, He rescued Lot and tried to re-establish him on a mountain. As Christians, we know what a mountain-top experience means, and that was what God wanted for Lot, but he chose to stay in the valley. Unlike us humans, who keep people we have forgiven at arm's length, God's second chance always puts people in a better position than they were before their failure.

In most cases, when God rights our wrongs, He tries to give us an opportunity for a fresh start. This time, He would want us to be perfect or do better going forward, just as He advised Abraham, except for Lot, who opted for the valley of Sodom instead of a fresh start on the mountain. We know how Lot's story ended.

# CHAPTER SIX

## *Christ, the Universal Truth*

The cliché, "all religions are the same," is becoming common among professed Christians, particularly in the Western world. Interestingly, Christians who are fond of this cliché are often loud about it, but when you pay closer attention to those who use this phrase, you will notice they are self-acclaimed Christians who do not see commitment and a personal relationship with Christ as a necessity.

A Christian is someone who is a follower of Christ, believes in His teachings, and accepts His offer of salvation wholeheartedly. No matter how we phrase it, God cannot be said to accept anything and everything as worship. Since all these religions making truth claims contradict each other, it is pertinent to state that only one, or none, of these truth claims can be true and universal.

So, which truth is universal?

For the sake of argument, among others, there are three main religions that compete side by side with each other.

- Christianity
- Islam
- Buddhism

In order to put this argument into proper context, I will begin my discourse with Buddhism. The central belief of Buddhism is often referred to as reincarnation, the concept that people are reborn after dying. In fact, the foundation of Buddhism is that most individuals go through many cycles of birth, life, death, and rebirth. Buddhists take karma seriously, as it is a fundamental principle that explains how our actions, thoughts, and intentions lead to consequences, both in this life and potentially in future lives.

This central belief forms the three Universal truths that define the Buddhist beliefs:

i.　Nothing is lost in the universe
ii.　Everything Changes
iii.　The Law of Cause and Effect (karma)

There is a general consensus among religious scholars, including Buddhists, that Buddha was not a god and the philosophy of Buddhism does not involve any theistic worldview. Therefore, the central focus of Buddhism is aimed solely at liberating sentient beings from suffering.

Since Buddhism does not advocate heaven or God, but only focuses on the ability of humans to overcome earthly sufferings, it is therefore sufficient to say that Buddhism and Christianity are not the same.

Christianity placed its central focus on God through Christ, while Buddhism has no business with God. Meaning, these two religions are not the same in any sense. With Buddhism out of the argument we are now left with Christianity and Islam.

Of all the different religions, Christianity and Islam are the only two religions that share some good degree of similarity in their beliefs. Unfortunately, these two religions cannot be said to be the same because the central focus of their worship are fundamentally different.

(Quran- Sura:66:12 states that Jesus was born when the spirit of God breathed upon Mary, whose body was chaste. When Christ was born, Allah kept his birth a secret and hid him: So she [Maryam] conceived him, and she withdrew with him to a remote place[19:22]).

Even though the Quran confirmed the greatness of Jesus Christ as a great Prophet born by a virgin and referred to Him as the word and spirit of God, the Quran also emphatically said Jesus is not the son of God and not God.

But Jesus Himself said He is the son of God and that He is God (John 14: 9), and no one comes to God but through Him (John 41:6). Though many who disagree with the appellation of Christ as the only way to God, attributes Christ's claim of being the light, the only truth and the only way to God as a statement of absolutism.

These two fundamental differences make it clear that these two religions are in no way the same because they fundamentally contradict each other.

The law of non-contradiction states that two contradictory statements cannot both be true at the same time and in the same sense or context. Therefore, these two religions cannot both be correct because they fundamentally contradict each other. Either Prophet Muhammad is right, and Jesus Christ is wrong in His claim of being the Son of God, or Jesus Christ is right in His claim of being the Son of God, and Prophet Muhammad is wrong.

## The Centric Cycle

Fraternal organizations like the Rosicrucian, Ekankar, Grail Message, and others, who equally believe in reincarnation like Buddhists, may disagree with Christianity in a number of ways, but all have arrived at the same conclusion: Christ is the only being who completed the centric circle (the number of times a person visits the Earth before reaching paradise) in one earthly visit.

The belief of these fraternal organizations is that they must strive to attain the qualities that qualify a person to enter paradise, which are achieved through cycles of birth and rebirth. Some individuals may go through this cycle thousands of times before they become pure enough to enter paradise. However, Christ completed this process in one earthly visit, confirming that He was without sin.

Even though Christianity does not share the view of these fraternal organizations, one pertinent question remains: If the central focus of all these fraternal organizations is to live an upright life on Earth to reduce the number of their earthly visits (as opposed to thousands of visits before they make it to paradise), why then do they not put their faith in the Man who smashed the record and completed the centric circle in one earthly visit?

This is because people are set in their ways, they have been behaving in the same way for many years and do not want to change.

Therefore, the one universal truth is Christ, because His life and teachings transcend different faiths. He is acknowledged in Islam as a child born of a virgin, a great Prophet with profound teachings, who performed many miracles and will return. Fraternal organizations speak of Him as the only being who completed the centric circle in a single earthly visit, because He was without sin throughout His life on earth.

Even King Nebuchadnezzar, a heathen king, recognized Christ when he saw Him in the fire alongside the three Hebrew children. Interestingly, this incident happened even before the birth of Christ (Daniel 3:25). For anyone reading this who believes there is a God but feels offended by the idea that Jesus was the Son of God and that no one comes to the Father but through Christ, you can pray to God to reveal Himself to you and enlighten you about the person of Jesus Christ. Many people from other faiths, or Christians who doubt and question whether Christ is real, are finding the answers they seek as Christ appears to be revealing Himself to them.

Apart from His great teachings and miracles, Jesus Christ died, resurrected, and was seen by over five hundred of His followers. He wasn't just a ghost operating in thin air; He became a body, no longer limited by space and time. That was why He was able to join His disciples while they were in a locked room. Thomas felt His wounds, and He broke bread with the disciples he met on the road to Emmaus (Luke 24:13-35). Even His mother's son, James, who seemed to think very little of Him as the Son of God before the crucifixion, became His disciple after He resurrected and fulfilled the prophecies. Heaven also opened to confirm His Sonship (Mark 9:7).

Christ is still manifesting Himself to this day, and people who have seen Christ, regardless of their religion, have never mistaken Him for Buddha, Muhammad, or other religious prophets.

So, if Jesus Christ tells you that no one comes to God but through Him alone, why don't you believe Him?

# CHAPTER SEVEN

## *Christ and Religion*

Religion is a collective way of worship. Therefore, religion is not solely about Christianity, as it can also be attributed to Islam, Hinduism, Buddhism, or other forms of worship or belief. Suffice it to say that these religions have established ways of worship. However, some individuals, particularly within Christianity, have chosen to redefine how worship can be observed by introducing their own political theocracy.

Christ is the central focus of Christianity. However, the term "Christianity" has been broadened by some to include those who attend church but do not wholeheartedly believe in the teachings of Christ, especially as they relate to how we manage our daily affairs or His claim of being the Way, the Truth, and the Life.

We are faced with a world where the church is competing and trying to be more secular than the world itself. Many of those cheering for secularism within the church still run around brandishing the Christian banner. While I am not in a position to judge them, their actions fall short of what is expected of Christians. Therefore, they are not true Christians. After all, Richard Dawkins, who still denies the existence of God, recently called himself a "cultural Christian." His idea of cultural Christianity is that he likes the morals preached by Christians, but does not believe there is a God anywhere. There is, therefore, a need to deconstruct the term "Christianity," as it now means different things to different people.

Christianity is much more than charity. It is much more than receiving praise from the council or the government for charitable projects executed, and it is more than being considered a "nice person." These actions are part of the second commandment of Christ (Mathew 22:39, thou shalt love thy neighbour as thyself). However, the first commandment, which Christ described as the greatest (Matthew 22:37, "Thou shalt love the Lord thy God with all thy heart, and with all thy soul, and with all thy mind"), takes priority and must not be compromised.

It is worth noting that when the second commandment takes over our focus, without being driven or shaped by the first commandment, our service to God becomes futile.

Showing love to a fellow human being is encouraged by God, because there is no way we can love God, whom we cannot see, if we do not love our neighbor (Matthew 25:35-36, "I was hungry and you gave Me food; I was thirsty and you gave Me drink; I was a stranger and you took Me in; I was naked and you clothed Me; I was sick and you visited Me; I was in prison and you visited Me"). Christ went further to state (Matthew 25:45, "Truly I say to you, to the extent that you did it to one of the least of these brothers, you did it to Me").

This view of Christ in relation to charity emphasizes the importance God attaches to love for one's neighbor. After all, God was drawn to Cornelius for his kindness to the poor.

However, if we do all the charitable works mentioned by Christ but doubt the Bible, disagree with God's view on morality, or reject the Bible's position on true and acceptable worship, then we are no different from those who do not believe in God.

## Light in the Last Days

The Bible has always been consistent if we give it the right context. Let's take, for example, Genesis 18:19: "For I know him, that he will command his children and his household after him, and they shall keep the way of the LORD." The Bible, in Proverbs 22:6, says, "Train up a child in the way he should go; even when he is old, he will not depart from it."

We can say these are all Old Testament views on holding onto what we have learned about God. In Luke 10:41-42 [NIV]. 41 "Martha, Martha," the Lord answered, "you are worried and upset about many things, 42 but few things are needed, or indeed only one.[a] Mary has chosen what is better, and it will not be taken away from her." Mary was trying to make her guest, Christ, comfortable, which was a charitable act, but Christ was saying, "Mary, focus on Me."

For those of us that have been fortunate to come to Christ, all the above are saying the same thing: "Stay the course."

In the story of Mary and Martha, Jesus generalizes this message, and it's not just about children as in the case of Abraham. What matters most is that the Bible is saying there is a possibility we might depart from our relationship with God, which could be the result of our personal choices or life's pressures. Christ used the phrase, "It will not be taken away from her," meaning that other circumstances can make us lose our relationship with God. However, Christ is saying that the more we know about God, the less likely this will happen.

God knows what He expects of us; He knows what manner of worship and service He expects from us. God is not Isaac, who could be deceived.

Genesis 27:22 [NIV]. Jacob went close to his father Isaac, who touched him and said, "The voice is the voice of Jacob, but the hands are the hands of Esau."

God did not accept the strange fire from the sons of Aaron, nor did He tolerate Uzzah when he attempted to steady the Ark of the Covenant. The two incidents mentioned here resulted in the death of people during their service to God, confirming that God does not accept anything and everything as service.

If we say that, because we are in the dispensation of grace, everything is acceptable to God, this is not true. That is why Christ cursed the fig tree. The fig tree represents the body of Esau and the voice of Jacob, it looks fruitful, but it bears no fruit. Christ was clear in His emphasis on the need for an acceptable service.

Matthew 7:22 -24 [NIV]. 22 "Many will say to me on that day, 'Lord, Lord, did we not prophesy in your name and in your name drive out demons and, in your name, perform many miracles?' 23 Then I will tell them plainly, 'I never knew you. Away from me, you evildoers!' The Wise and Foolish Builders. 24 "Therefore, everyone who hears these words of mine and puts them into practice is like a wise man who built his house on the rock".

Consequently, the key and primary criterion for making it to heaven is believing wholeheartedly in Christ as the Son of God. We must believe in His teachings on how we should live our lives. Our service in the church and our charitable works toward fellow humans should come as an addition (Matthew 7:21, "Not everyone who says to me, 'Lord, Lord,' will enter the kingdom of heaven, but only the one who does the will of my Father who is in heaven"). Jesus went further to state (Matthew 7:23, "And I will declare to them, 'I never knew you; depart from me, you who practice lawlessness'").

In some countries, priests often focus their messages on community service, sharing, and loving one another, leaving out the first and most important commandment of Jesus Christ: "You must love the Lord your God with all your heart and all your strength."

I'm not suggesting that we should intentionally offend or upset people in the name of preaching the Gospel. However, if you believe that the word of God should always be preached in a way that leaves everyone feeling good about themselves, then you might want to reflect on the words of Archbishop Oscar Romero, the Catholic martyr, who famously questioned "what kind of gospel is preached when it doesn't touch the real sins of society. He argued that a church that doesn't provoke crisis, a gospel that doesn't disturb, and a word of God that doesn't get under anyone's skin, is not a true reflection of God's love and power."

The word of God is not always about comfort; sometimes it heals and soothes a troubled heart, and at other times, it is meant to make us uncomfortable enough to inspire change in us. This isn't about preaching hate; no matter how nicely the word is presented, it is designed to provoke change in us. Drivers feel uneasy when they see a diversion sign ahead, even if the sign is asking them to change course because there are possible problems in the direction they are headed.

The idea of salvation through Christ can seem exhausting to some because they forget that the Christian walk is all about trusting Christ as we go about our daily activities. The power to live for God comes from God. All we need to do is connect to that heavenly frequency, which will help keep us on track.

So much moral burden has been placed on Christians, which is why the world is quick to criticize and pick apart their actions. This same moral burden is not placed on those of other faiths, which further reinforces the view that it is only through the Christian faith that humanity will find salvation.

We have been called to be the salt and the light of the world and the tool to do this is the word of God. Salt preserves and prevents decay, and the need for preservation arises from the tendency for deterioration.

Light, in itself, exposes anything hidden in the dark. The dark might represent secret sins or habits in our lives, some of the struggles that others don't know about. Even Christians sometimes carry certain habits around and are oblivious to them as sinful. Habits like envy, gossip, unforgiveness, and pride, which are often overlooked as insignificant, can grab our attention when the word of God shines a light on them.

Being the salt of the earth requires balance. Just like salt, if the soup is too salty, it becomes inedible; if there is not enough salt, the soup becomes tasteless. Therefore, we need to find that balance so we don't drive people away from God while seasoning our world. We need the daily guidance of the Holy Spirit and godly wisdom to achieve this balance.

We can only achieve this by first living out the word of God, the life Christ preached, and also preaching the good news to provoke a change in people. We are not called to be zealots who think they are good and others are bad. We have been called to preach Christ and allow the Holy Spirit to convict people and draw them to Christ.

Sometimes, only a word sown into a person's heart is enough to bring them into the kingdom. On other occasions, we might be required to persevere with people by repeating our message to bring them to the point of conviction. There are people who have been preached to and walked away, only to give their life to Christ a year later or six months later, even when no other message was preached to them. The good news is a seed, once sown, it can bring life when certain life events occur. Suddenly, the thought of giving God a chance becomes the only burden in the person's heart, and that is how the Holy Spirit works.

As Christians, we represent Christ. We are ambassadors, not judges. Ambassadors do not judge the people they live amongst but pursue the interests of the country they represent. We represent heaven, and we can't judge people into the kingdom. Our role is to bring the word, while it is the Holy Spirit's role to convict people.

## Light in the Last Days

Matthew 5:13 [NIV]: "You are the salt of the earth. But if the salt loses its saltiness, how can it be made salty again? It is no longer good for anything, except to be thrown out and trampled underfoot."

Not being too salty to the point of being corrosive does not necessarily mean we should be saltless to the point of being tasteless. Unfortunately, many Christians have lost their salt as each one chooses their own morality.

Politicians tell the world the mind of the people (their constituency), but priests tell the world the mind of God. Unfortunately, many priests no longer shine a light on acts the Bible (God) considers sinful, just to avoid backlash from members of their congregation. What then is the role of the priest if not to tell the world that God loves you and wants you to come as you are, but that this act is sinful, and that act is sinful?

Let's look at the story of the woman with the issue of blood. Back then, when a woman was having her monthly cycle, she was considered unclean, but this woman touched Jesus while in her unclean state and received her healing. When Christ realized that virtue had gone out of Him, He turned and asked, "Who touched me?" She was terrified, as she knew she should not have done this because she was unclean. Christ did not rebuke her for touching Him while she was in her unclean state because He wants us to come as we are. He called her "daughter" and said her faith had healed her before asking her to go in peace.

Many times, we want to better ourselves before coming to God, and in most cases, all our efforts to get it right end in failure. People do not visit the pharmacist after they are healed, they visit them while they are still sick and unwell. So it is with our need for Christ, He wants us to come to Him while we are still in sin and unclean, because He has the power to make everything new again.

Let's consider another story where Jesus forgives and heals a paralyzed man in Luke 5:17-25 [NIV]: "17 One day Jesus was teaching, and Pharisees and teachers of the law were sitting there. They had come from every village of Galilee and from Judea and Jerusalem. And the power of the Lord was with Jesus to heal the sick. 18 Some men came carrying a paralyzed man on a mat and tried to take him into the house to lay him before Jesus. 19 When they could not find a way to do this because of the crowd, they went up on the roof and lowered him on his mat through the tiles into the middle of the crowd, right in front of Jesus.

20 When Jesus saw their faith, He said, "Friend, your sins are forgiven."

21 The Pharisees and the teachers of the law began thinking to themselves, "Who is this fellow who speaks blasphemy? Who can forgive sins but God alone?"

22 Jesus knew what they were thinking and asked, "Why are you thinking these things in your hearts? 23 Which is easier: to say, 'Your sins are forgiven,' or to say, 'Get up and walk'? 24 But I want you to know that the Son of Man has authority on earth to forgive sins." So He said to the paralyzed man, "I tell you, get up, take your mat, and go home." 25 Immediately, he stood up in front of them, took what he had been lying on, and went home praising God."

The Pharisees were, in fact, correct in stating that only God has the authority to forgive sins. The tragedy, however, was their failure to recognize that they were speaking to God Himself. Their criticism wasn't necessarily invalid, it simply overlooked a deeper truth. Judgment ultimately belongs to God. In the parable of the prodigal son, the father did not argue that the elder son's accusations were false. Instead, he reminded him that it was his prerogative to decide how to respond to the one who had erred.

Jesus did not rebuke these friends for their desperation, for going so far as to lower their sick friend through the roof just for Christ to heal him. Instead, He commended their faith. God has love for us, but this love can be rekindled and strengthened by the kind of faith we show, particularly the faith that says, "Lord, I am helpless, please help me."

Christ Himself is love, but we shouldn't focus solely on Christ being love. Rather, we should place our faith in Him as the only way to eternal life, and apply His teachings in how we deal with our daily affairs. When Christians move away from religion, which can be considered ambiguous, and develop a more defined relationship with Christ, the Church as a body will be quickened to fulfill the purpose for which Christ died.

Moreover, there is no such thing as, "I do what I can, and God understands the rest." Our love for God should be reflected in the views we uphold. God knows whether we uphold His views or not, we can't deceive Him.

C.S. Lewis describes two types of people: the first are those who bend their knees to God and say to Him, "Your will be done," and the second are those who refuse to bend their knee to God, and God says to them, "Your will be done."

Consequently, religion can undergo collective metamorphosis but relationship with Christ does not metamorphose on a collective basis. Relationships with Christ can only grow on a personal level. There can be a mass revival, yet spiritual experiences are on a personal level.

# CHAPTER EIGHT

## *Christ and other prophets*

Many of the prophets who came before Jesus performed miracles similar to those Christ did.

Elisha and Elijah didn't walk on water, but they both parted the Jordan (2 Kings 2:1-14). They both raised the dead, just as Christ did. Like Enoch, Elijah did not die, he was taken up in a chariot. Christ, too, ascended to heaven, and this is something that Christ, Enoch, and Elijah have in common. If other religious faiths do not talk about these prophets of God, Islam does.

Islam refers to these prophets as great prophets, but none of them is described as the "Word and Spirit of God." Islam, however, describes Christ as the "Word and Spirit of God," and when Christ says He is the Word of God, it means that everything He says carries the power of God. Everything God created was made through His Word, and that Word happens to be Christ, as even acknowledged by the Islamic faith. Therefore, if the same Christ, acknowledged as the Word of God, tells you anything about the Father, it is logical to believe Christ.

Aside from Christ being the active force of creation, as the Word of God that brought everything into being, there are other events peculiar to Christ. The tearing of the temple curtain after

His death ended the exclusivity of the priesthood's access to the throne of grace, giving everyone access to God. After His death, darkness fell over the land, and the graves opened, with the dead rising. This signifies hope for the dead. It is therefore safe to conclude that Christ is not just a wise teacher, a sage, or a prophet, but God Himself. Unlike other prophets, Christ forgave people of their sins, a prerogative He uniquely exercised. What about the prophecies of His birth, death, and the famous entry into Jerusalem three days before His death?

God has long been presenting Christ to us in different events and circumstances, even before His birth. In all these circumstances, the message has always been the same: "You don't have to fight to save yourself, I will save you."

From the story of the three Hebrew children to the death and resurrection of Christ, we can see the consistency of Christ's saving grace. Christ entered the fire to save the three Hebrew children, and they did not fight the fire. His presence alone preserved them. On the night of the Passover, Christ was the lamb on the doorpost. The Israelites didn't have to fight to save themselves from the wrath of the angel of death sweeping through Egypt; the blood on the doorpost did the job of preservation.

In the wilderness, when the Israelites were plagued by snake bites, God instructed Moses to lift up the bronze serpent on a cross, symbolizing Christ crucified. If the people looked at the bronze serpent, they would live, meaning they did not have to fight the snakes or find a cure for the snake bites to stay alive. All they needed to do was look at the bronze serpent, and Christ's saving grace would do the rest. When Peter stepped out of the boat and walked on water, he succeeded as long as his focus was on Christ, but the moment he focused on the wind, he began to sink.

Let's take this further back to Abraham's encounter with Melchizedek in Genesis 14. This will give us better insight into how Christ shows up and intervenes in the affairs of God's people. We will also notice that the first difficult physical battle Abraham faced was against the kings of Shinar, Ellasar, Elam, and Goyim. It was when Abraham was returning from this war that he encountered Melchizedek. The Bible does not mention Melchizedek's participation in that war, but I am convinced that Melchizedek went with Abraham for that war, perhaps in spirit.

In all the events mentioned above, which occurred hundreds of years apart, Christ's saving power was manifest in saving people from physical death. He has always shown up in one way or another through time, which makes Christ unique compared to any other being, prophet, or man.

Finally, we will consider the present dispensation, which is tied to the spiritual realm, and this is the ultimate. When Adam and Eve sinned against God, they died spiritually, but a relationship with Christ can save a life destined for death, just as we have observed in the past.

Today, if we acknowledge His Lordship, we will be saved from the spiritual death we all inherited. Similarly, we do not have to do anything to be alive spiritually other than believe and put our faith in Christ as our only Savior.

Roman 8:3-6 [NIV]. "3 For what the law was powerless to do because it was weakened by the flesh,[b] God did by sending his own Son in the likeness of sinful flesh to be a sin offering.[c] And so he condemned sin in the flesh, 4 in order that the righteous requirement of the law might be fully met in us, who do not live according to the flesh but according to the Spirit. 5 Those who live according to the flesh have their minds set on what the flesh desires; but those who live in accordance with the Spirit have their minds set on what the Spirit desires. 6 The mind governed by the flesh is death, but the mind governed by the Spirit is life and peace."

*Light in the Last Days*

In verse 5, the bible says, Those who live according to the flesh have their minds set on what the flesh desires; but those who live in accordance with the Spirit have their minds set on what the Spirit desires.

The Bible speaks extensively about the carnal man, one who lives according to the flesh, and why such a life is at odds with God. In Romans 8:7 (KJV), it says, "Because the carnal mind is enmity against God." And in verse 8, it adds, "So then they that are in the flesh cannot please God." Sadly, many unbelievers and even believers, fail to reflect on how much Scripture warns about the power the flesh holds over humanity.

"Let's pause and consider what the 'flesh,' our body, truly represents in our lives as humans."

We eat and drink to sustain our bodies. We dress to cover them, sometimes to stay warm to preserve them, and often to appear presentable and attractive just to make ourselves look good. We live in houses so our bodies aren't exposed to the elements or left without shelter. At night, we lock our doors to protect both our bodies and our possessions, possessions that, in most cases, serve the needs of the body.

We drive comfortable cars and sleep in cozy beds to please the body. We work and earn money primarily to care for our physical needs. Even the person who invented the product we use likely did so with the intention of making money, ultimately to provide for their own body. When we travel by air, road, or rail, it's our body we're transporting. When we watch TV or listen to music, we're entertaining the senses of the body.

Consider the first 22 years or more of a person's life, spent in education, from nursery through university, all with the aim of securing employment, ultimately to provide for the body. Some go further, pursuing master's or doctorate degrees, seeking better financial rewards for the same purpose. Even acts of financial support toward others often stem from a desire to help them maintain or improve their physical well-being.

At a busy bus or train station, you'll see crowds of people rushing off to different destinations. Some are well-dressed, others not as much, but all are pursuing one thing: a way to satisfy the demands of the flesh. All the toiling of our lives is ultimately aimed at taking care of our bodies. The flesh resists accountability, hides wrongdoing, and constantly seeks comfort, pleasure, and self-justification.

Therefore, if a person spends two decades or more of their lives pursuing education, subconsciously with the sole intention of getting a good job just to take care of their flesh, it means that, whether consciously or subconsciously, it becomes easier to justify compromising values or engaging in ungodly actions, just to meet the flesh's demands.

Although we are no longer under the law, to live a victorious Christian life requires intentionality. We must understand the desires of the flesh and resist them by setting Christ as our daily standard.

Living the Christian life doesn't need to be a struggle if we are led by the Holy Spirit. When guided by Him, we no longer feel the need to cheat for financial gain, lie for acceptance, or dress immodestly to attract attention. Our speech becomes gracious, not provoking conflict or division.

God, our Creator, understands that every man is a fallen creation following the fall of Adam and Eve. It is God's desire that we be reconciled to Him, and it is important to God that our hearts are right by the time we are reconciled to Him. Most of Christ's messages focused on the human heart. Proverbs 4:23 says, "Above all else, guard your heart, for everything you do flows from it." Jeremiah 17:9 [NIV] says, "The heart is deceitful above all things and beyond cure. Who can understand it?" In many instances, Christ moved the conversation beyond our outward actions and placed emphasis on the heart, addressing issues like unforgiveness and acts of sexual immorality. In truth, the central concept of Christianity is predicated on the human heart.

Pastor Yomi Olowoyo once said, "The consequence of not guarding your heart can be poor choices, broken relationships, hurt, and disappointment. But remember, when we mess up and are not the best version of ourselves, God is faithful to forgive and restore."

Christ's earthly mission is primarily about conquering the human heart. According to the Bible, multitudes fall on their faces before the throne and cry out in praise to God. The saints in heaven worship God through prayer, song, and other acts of reverence. The 24 elders fall down before God's throne and worship Him. If this level of reverence to God is what happens in heaven, then God would not want anyone whose heart is not right to be in heaven. This is not a place for someone full of pride, seeking reverence for themselves instead of giving reverence to God. All other prophets came to point us to God, but Christ, on the other hand, came to point us to Himself. In all of this, Christ wants us to surrender our sovereignty and rely wholly on Him.

As opposed to establishing an earthly kingdom, Christ wants to be the King of our hearts. He will not barge into our hearts, we are expected to invite Him in. It is evident that Christ is still showing up in the lives of people today, just as He did for thousands of years, either to save some from physical death in life-and-death situations, or from spiritual death through the offer of salvation.

Many Christians, including those of other faiths, have testified to their encounters with Christ. While some encountered Him physically, others experienced Him through trance or dreams. In all of these cases, He comes to address specific concerns that make it clear He is the one who revealed Himself to us or stepped into that situation for us.

# CHAPTER NINE

## *The "Do Not Judge" Slogan*

Recent research reveals that religion can be as intoxicating as alcohol. This is because it shapes a person's perspective on various issues, regardless of the nature of the matter at hand. Whether it be scientific, social, environmental, moral, or even simple numerical issues, a person with deep religious affiliation responds to these matters from the perspective of their faith.

People with strong religious convictions can sometimes seem insensitive or judgmental. However, these individuals are not zealots or fanatics; they are ordinary Christians who base their contributions in conversations on their understanding of God.

The slogan "do not judge" has become a common cliché many Christians use to shut down others who try to admonish them or point out the excesses of others. This slogan has essentially become a "shut up" card. Many within the body of Christ have grown hesitant to offer counsel to fellow believers, fearing they'll be accused of being judgmental. This brings to mind the saying: no one wants to be the one to tell the emperor he's wearing no clothes, for fear of incurring his anger.

The truth is, judgment is reserved for God, and we are not in a position to judge others or suggest what punishment may await them. Even Christ Himself encourages us to remove the logs from our own eyes before pointing out the specks in the eyes of others.

As Christians, we can't be both a judge and a savior at the same time. Our role is to bring people to salvation, which implies that the role of a judge is not ours. The question, then, is: Are we allowed to admonish fellow Christians, particularly when they are going astray?

The Christian journey is much more than children in a playground not speaking to each other after a fight. The Bible says, "Iron sharpens iron," and because even the best of us can miss the mark, treating the journey as a collective cause becomes essential.

Luke 17:3 (ESV): "Pay attention to yourselves! If your brother sins, rebuke him, and if he repents, forgive him."

Christ's advice on how we should relate to a brother or sister who has fallen into sin involves getting involved in the other person's life and pointing out their flaws. The word "rebuke" may seem strong, but even if we substitute it with a more subtle word like "correct," the context of the verse still calls for admonishing others over their sinful actions. Unfortunately, pointing out someone else's sin may lead to them accusing you of being judgmental, without considering the sinful lifestyle in question.

Christ also emphasized that we should pay attention to ourselves, so we don't fall victim to pride or become tempted to hold offense against the person we intend to correct.

Arguably, people who share a common cause can be expected to hold each other accountable. This is why siblings, close friends, and colleagues at work might admonish one another in the context of their shared interest in each other's well-being and positive behavior within the group.

In my view, the word of God is enough to speak for itself and prompt someone to change their course, if they so desire.

Interestingly, a word from God doesn't just come out of thin air, it must come from the brethren.

Therefore, when the Bible says "iron sharpens iron" in Proverbs 27:17, it's not just talking about good friends helping each other grow. It also points to the friction involved in the sharpening process. When one piece of iron sharpens another, there's friction, there's noise, and there are sparks.

So, in the context of Christian faith, "iron sharpening iron" means that growth often comes through discomfort. One person may challenge or correct another, not out of judgment, but out of love and that process can still be uncomfortable. The truth is, you can't sharpen iron without friction. Likewise, we must understand that loving correction might still cause discomfort, and that's okay. It's part of being sharpened and made better.

Hebrews 4:12, "For the word of God is alive and active. Sharper than any double-edged sword, it penetrates even to divide soul and spirit, joints and marrow; it judges the thoughts and attitudes of the heart."

Considering the above scripture, it is evident that advice or admonishment based on the word of God will shed light on the errors in our lives, particularly where our lifestyle does not align with God's will. The word of God also provokes a reaction that can lead us to change course. For example, Christ healed the sick man by the pool of Bethsaida and then told him to sin no more.

Many of us can't bear being told that our actions or lifestyle are sinful. We often attribute such rebuke, no matter how subtle or modest, to being judged or condemned by a self-righteous Christian. In most cases, the way we live our lives and react to issues shows that "we draw the line and want God to fall in line." But in reality, God draws the line, and we must fall in line. We can choose whether or not to follow, but God knows His line.

*Light in the Last Days*

The focus should not be on feeling condemned or judged, because both Christians and non-Christians alike will, at some point, realize that their actions are wrong. Even good Christians sometimes struggle with sin, whether it's how we handle our anger or even the lust in our hearts. In fact, true Christians deal with sin by self-reflecting and removing themselves from circumstances that lead to sin.

God does not accept everything and anything. Even our human society is guided by standards (for instance, there are fitness standards in the military, behavior expectations in the medical profession, and set standards in other professions). If human society has standards, how then can we assume that God has none?

My friend Dan has always reminded me that it was because of the way Christians behaved that his mother left the church. I felt bad when I heard this and told him I was sorry to hear that his mother had to leave because of the actions of others. However, as we discussed the issue further, I realized that his mother expected everyone else in the church to be perfect and forgiving while excusing her own aggression toward other members.

Interestingly, the saint you might expect to see in the church could be someone who started attending just two weeks ago, someone who has lived most of their life on the streets, doing drugs, or someone whose life was a complete mess.

I also made Dan understand that the church is not a place where perfect people congregate but a place where people come to work out their own salvation. It is important to note that the world expects more from the church, and people should find comfort and hope there without being judged. However, the problem with the mentality Dan had was that others were expected to change, while it was his right to remain the way he was. Unfortunately, this is not Christ's position. Christ wants us to come as we are but expects us to grow.

Dan himself moves from job to job, finding it difficult to hold onto a position because of his inability to co-exist with colleagues. To Dan, every other person is wrong, and he alone is right, a trait he shares with his mom, blaming others for the issues.

We are expected to grow in our actions, perceptions about life, and attitudes toward others. If the Christian faith is about blessing those who despise us, praying for those who persecute us, loving our neighbor as ourselves, healing the sick, being of good cheer, giving food to the hungry, and drink to the thirsty, who wouldn't want to be intoxicated with such a faith?

Imagine how wonderful the world would be if we all genuinely allowed ourselves to be intoxicated with the Christian faith. In reality, these fruits flow from God. I don't mind being intoxicated with my Christian beliefs, provided my life is associated with love, joy, peace, patience, kindness, goodness, faithfulness, gentleness, and self-control.

What kind of world are we advocating if, as a society, we welcome the church's intervention in our political life to tackle issues like poverty, persecution, and war, but consider it pervasive when the church encourages us to let God's morals influence how we live our lives?

Journalists are eager to hear not only the views but also the opinions of religious leaders on poverty, war, political unrest, and suffering in general. However, they often forget that every crisis facing the world today is a consequence of the thoughts in the human heart.

Jesus Christ didn't judge, but that does not mean He didn't call out the hypocrisy of the Pharisees. He called the Pharisees "devourers of widows" because their secret lives did not represent the values they claimed to uphold publicly. John 8:10-11: "Then Jesus straightened up and asked her, 'Woman, where are your accusers? Has no one condemned you?' 'No one, Lord,' she answered. 'Then neither do

*Light in the Last Days*

I condemn you,' Jesus declared. "Now go and sin no more." In the same way, Christ did not condemn the woman charged with adultery, but He emphatically told her to "sin no more," meaning her actions were sinful.

Pastor Yomi Olowoyo of Christian life Centre Thamesmead said, "you don't go looking for the devil, but if he shows up, kick him out." This advice is for Christians who are overly fixated on the errors or sins of others. Please note that many people in the body of Christ are there to work out their salvation. However, we are not expected to remain the same forever. The Bible says, "To whom much is given, much is expected" (Luke 12:48). Our behavior and lifestyle must reflect the words of God that we have received over the years. Christ is archetypal of God; therefore, instead of focusing on the errors of Christians working out their own salvation, we should focus on Christ.

Furthermore, admonishing, commenting on, and pointing out moral breakdowns or inconsistencies in the faith does not mean you are judging others. Rather, you are merely asserting the position of your faith as it relates to the matter at hand. This should not be interpreted as condemnation. We should not make a habit of looking for faults in others or criticizing the faith. Such criticism does not help the faith, it does not bring people into the faith. On the contrary, it makes people leave.

Christ's mission is not about blaming people for their pasts. Regardless of how ugly our pasts may be, Christ is only interested in changing our past by giving us a new future. He emphatically stated that He came for the sick, not for those whose lives are perfect. Unfortunately, no life is perfect, even for those who perceive themselves as having a perfect life, but sometimes the destructive actions of some Christians are just too obvious to be ignored.

The mess created by some so-called men of God is as obvious as a child in a candy store who cannot stop breaking things and this does not help. There is no denying the fact that there are charlatans, impostors, and false prophets out there, masquerading as pastors. This should not surprise us, as the Bible has already captured the story of a man wanting to pay for the gifts of the Spirit in Peter, intending to use them for profit.

Acts 8:18-21 [NIV]. 18 "When Simon saw that the Spirit was given at the laying on of the apostles' hands, he offered them money 19 and said, "Give me also this ability so that everyone on whom I lay my hands may receive the Holy Spirit." 20 Peter answered: "May your money perish with you, because you thought you could buy the gift of God with money! 21 You have no part or share in this ministry, because your heart is not right before God."

Christ himself talked about this in the bible book Matthew 7:22-23 (NKJV). "Many will say to Me in that day, "Lord, Lord, have we not...done many wonders in Your name?" And then I will declare to them, "I never knew you; depart from Me".

The bible confirms how narrow the right path is, which confirms the fact that many are not on the right path. Matthew 7:13-14 [NIV]. 13 "Enter through the narrow gate. For wide is the gate and broad is the road that leads to destruction, and many enter through it. 14 But small is the gate and narrow the road that leads to life, and only a few find it".

The verse above implies that only a tiny fraction of professing Christians will make it through the narrow gate.

Consequently, the question remains, should we lose our faith because of the erroneous practices of others? Certainly not. Excessive focus on the errors of others can easily lead a person into sin and possibly cause them to fall out of the faith. I have seen men of God who, after making mistakes, were exposed or came to a self-realization, decided to pick themselves up, go to God with a broken and contrite heart to ask for mercy, and eventually reconcile with God. Unfortunately, many who left the faith because of these men's wrongs never returned, but the man himself is back on track with God. The story of David and Bathsheba is a good example of this. David suffered the consequences of his actions, but his contrite heart and plea for forgiveness reconciled him with God.

There is nothing new under the sun. Whatever excuse we might give for isolating ourselves from the faith is not good enough. Whatever excuse we have today has already been captured in the Bible in one form or another, so it is not new. This does not necessarily mean we should continue associating with false teachings, rather, we should seek congregations where sound doctrine is being taught.

Being born again in Christ goes beyond simply having a kindred spirit. While a kindred spirit refers to someone who shares similar views or interests, being born again means becoming part of the same spiritual body, with Christ as the head. Just as the human body is made up of different parts, like the hand, leg, toe, and neck, each playing a unique role in supporting the health and function of the whole, so too every born-again believer has a distinct and essential place in the body of Christ.

Therefore, it is important not to forsake the assembly of the children of God. We cannot, because of the possibility that some men of God are not genuine or sincere, choose to isolate ourselves. We might erroneously think that we can study the word of God for ourselves without associating with any church. After all, the Bible encouraged us to study the word for ourselves, like the Bereans did. But this is not enough. Truth be told, if we isolate ourselves, we will become stale without even realizing it, because there is something about being in a congregation.

Unfortunately, we are living in a time when trust in institutions including the church, is at an all-time low. For those of you faithful Christians who may have fallen into sin after being disheartened by the mistakes of fellow believers, I encourage you to rise again and renew your relationship with Christ.

*Boniface Ossai*

Many times, when I find myself among unbelievers who are quick to point to scandals involving men of God as the reason they can't trust pastors, I tell them that Christ already said many people will not make it to heaven. I then ask if they trust Christ Himself and believe in His teachings, and of course, many of them often say they do. My next question is, do you want to miss heaven because some others are messing up their chances of making it? In most cases, the answer is, "No."

# CHAPTER TEN

## *The Ancient landmark, why this is necessary*

Landmarks are indicators, markers, or guiding lights that help us walk and work within a set boundary. There is no doubt that God is still working and revealing Himself to people in our day.

Aside from the teachings of Christ, the Christian faith sometimes makes reference to the work of fathers of the faith. These are Christian writers, theologians and great men of God who laid the doctrinal and intellectual groundwork for Christianity, most importantly the acts of the Apostles. These doctrinal groundwork now serves as landmarks that form the framework for our walk with God.

Many of us, for the sake of our own convenience, have moved the ancient landmarks. Over the years and in past centuries, the teachings of Apostle Paul were considered an authority, a model, and a foundation for doctrinal practices in our Christian faith.

In recent times, Christians seeking to pursue their own narrative and for their own convenience have sparked a debate that the teachings of Apostle Paul are his views on the various subjects he admonished the church about. They now argue that these are not the words of God, but rather the personal views of Apostle Paul. While we pursue innovative ways of doing things, it is important not to lose the crux of the good news, which is the resurrected Christ. God knew a time like this would come, particularly as an indication that we are in the last days.

While the Global West is so forward-looking, Christians in Africa are both forward-looking and backward-looking. The West has been credited with great men who toiled for the faith and successfully passed the burning torch, full of glow, to the generation succeeding them. People like John Wesley, Smith Wigglesworth, Oral Roberts, Catherine Kuhlman, Billy Graham, Kenneth Hagin... the list goes on, have proved their devotion to God, and the world can attest to this. Unfortunately, the West has suddenly become so forward-looking and in a hurry to extinguish the torch and erase every landmark left behind by these giants in the faith. Unlike the West, Africans always make decisions with full consideration of their history, culture, and past.

In today's West, the Christian faith has been characterized as some sort of Orwellian nightmare that runs contrary to Western values. There is every possibility that the word of God will make any person whose lifestyle is not aligned with God's uncomfortable. The good versus evil narrative has suddenly been used to cast the Christian faith as evil, as they now brand the good news as hate speech. This is where the idea of ascribing the good news to hate messages came from, further demonizing the Christian faith.

We want a perfect world but want the Creator to stay out of it. We want the blessing but hate the blesser. We want the gift but hate the giver of the gift. We hate pruning but want to look good at the same time, and may eventually grow wild. Many times, we underestimate the importance of maintaining and reinforcing ancient landmarks.

*Light in the Last Days*

The United Kingdom, as a nation, has in recent years made a conscious effort to disassociate itself from the Christian faith. This is a Christian nation that played a major role in spreading the gospel around the world.

Many have, for the sake of curiosity, questioned the motive behind the UK's missionary work around the world, as some associate it with slavery and empire-building. In earnest, if the motive was wrapped in deceit, then we will leave that to God to judge. However, the Christian faith itself is not fraudulent, as we can see churches and altars erected in their own land as a testament that they too believed in what they preached to nations at the ends of the earth. At this point, what matters most should not be how we perceive the motives of these missionaries, but that the good news of Christ was preached to the ends of the earth.

There are churches built and altars erected in every nook and cranny of the United Kingdom, reinforcing the argument that the UK is a Christian country. The popular King James Bible is a testament to the UK's contribution to the spread of the gospel. The Christian faith, once such a precious aspect of the United Kingdom, is today considered an anathema.

The United Kingdom is known to have produced several heroes who helped shape human civilization, and interestingly, most of these heroes attributed their success to God. One good example was Admiral Lord Nelson, whose final words after he was shot twice at the Battle of Trafalgar were not "Kiss me, Hardy," as was earlier thought. An unearthed letter has claimed that the British naval hero instead declared, "Thanks be to God," as he died after being shot twice during his victory over the French and Spanish at Trafalgar in 1805. Thanking God while taking his last breath after being shot shows the level of faith exercised by this hero and where he drew his strength from.

We have many angry people out there who feel they have no reason to give God thanks. People who believe God does not deserve a thank you from them, possibly because of their present circumstances. This admiral was not angry at God for allowing him to die at the age of 47, but he thanked God for the opportunity He gave him thus far. These weren't men using God for the purpose of exploiting others, these were men who truly believed in the God they preached.

As mentioned earlier, the translation of the Bible into the English language, now popularly known as the King James Bible, is one great achievement in the spread of the good news that is attributed to the United Kingdom.

Acts 21:10-13 [NIV]. "10 After we had been there a number of days, a prophet named Agabus came down from Judea. 11 Coming over to us, he took Paul's belt, tied his own hands and feet with it and said, "The Holy Spirit says, 'In this way the Jewish leaders in Jerusalem will bind the owner of this belt and will hand him over to the Gentiles. 12 When we heard this, we and the people there pleaded with Paul not to go up to Jerusalem. 13 Then Paul answered, "Why are you weeping and breaking my heart? I am ready not only to be bound, but also to die in Jerusalem for the name of the Lord Jesus."

The exceedingly great faith shown by Apostle Paul was the driving factor behind many pioneers of the Christian faith in the UK. People like Lord Nelson, and many others, including Mary Slessor, who died and was buried in Calabar, Nigeria, were inspired to become missionaries. Mary Slessor, in particular, was motivated to join the mission field after the death of her elder brother, who was also a missionary.

We can't talk about the role the UK played in the spread of the good news without mentioning names like Charles Spurgeon, the famous UK Christian preacher known as the 'Prince of Preachers,' who profoundly impacted Christianity through his powerful sermons and writings, and Charles Wesley, who wrote over 6,000 hymns, many of which we still sing in our churches today.

There are many other pioneers of the faith who died spreading the good news. The United Kingdom has so much to show for its Christian heritage, but this is not the case today.

What we see in the UK now are people in leadership positions who are quick to say they do not believe God exists. Unlike in the UK, United States presidents still proudly display their faith. They will openly tell you they are Catholic or Evangelical, even if their actions sometimes suggest otherwise, but at least they still associate themselves with the faith.

Currently in the UK, prime ministers and even members of the shadow cabinet not only distance themselves from the faith but are often quick to denounce God the moment they assume leadership roles. Unfortunately, the extent of their wisdom has led to a failing economy that we all see today.

Water always flows downstream. If the government itself is championing the crusade against the Christian faith, how then do we expect faith to grow in the land? Christ said He hopes He will find faith when He returns.

Today, there is a high level of anger and disaffection among the citizens of the United Kingdom as they worry about changing demographics in their country. The Bible says we should ask for the ancient path so we can walk in it, and our souls will find rest.

This disaffection has blossomed and resulted in citizens taking to the streets to protest what they see as a changing society. They want their country to resemble what it was many years ago, when the idea of kicking God out of the affairs of the nation was not at the forefront of the agenda.

As the saying goes, "Those whom the gods wish to destroy, they first make mad." What we are witnessing today is the result of a determined effort to sideline the Christian faith while other religions appear to gain greater acceptance.

Jeremiah 6:16 [NIV].16 This is what the LORD says: "Stand at the crossroads and look; ask for the ancient paths, ask where the good way is, and walk in it, and you will find rest for your souls. But you said, 'We will not walk in it.'"

Western society is beautiful, and what makes it unique is that it was founded on the Judeo-Christian religion. At least, it is common knowledge that people from other continents are clamoring for the kind of freedom and equality upon which Western society is built. The story of the three sisters who went to Moses to request to inherit their late father's assets, and God's response to their request, shows the heart of God.

In the Bible's Book of Numbers 27:1-11, the sisters argued that their father's name and lineage should not be cut off from his clan because he had no son. They asked to be allowed to inherit his land and property. Moses brought their case before God, who agreed with the sisters and instructed Moses to give them the property. God also went on to establish a new rule for inheritance, stating that when a man dies without a son, his daughters should inherit his property first, followed by his male relatives. This kind of fairness is what Western societies are known for.

Unfortunately, when we knock down the pillars of our national identity, we make ourselves a people without a belief. The United Kingdom is now a nation that stands for everything and represents nothing.

Someone once said, "A conversation you are supposed to have with God that you don't have with Him, Satan will have with you." Russell Brand was talking about the life he lived before he found Christ and said the awakening he experienced came from 1 Corinthians 6:19-20: "Do you not know that your body is a temple of the Holy Spirit, who is in you, whom you have received from

God? You are not your own." Russell Brand continued to echo the words, "Did you not know that your body is the temple?" He said these were the words that got to him.

Many people forget that there is no vacuum in the spirit realm. When you kick out your Christian faith, people of other faiths will come in and establish their own beliefs. The story of the madman of Gadara is an indication of how the spirit realm works.

The demonic forces within the madman recognized Christ's supremacy and understood that their time of using him as a host had come to an end, as a greater power had intervened. The moment the demons were cast out, the madman was instantly filled with the light of Christ. The same principle applies in reverse, if the Spirit of God departs from a person's life, the devil will quickly take over that space.

When Esau moved the ancient landmark, God did not waste His time on Esau but turned to his brother, Jacob. Esau later found himself begging and crying to get back what belonged to him, which was his position as the heir, but he didn't get it.

Esau did not move the ancient landmark on the day he sold his birthright to his brother for a pot of red pottage. He moved the landmark by marrying two Edomite women, something God had forbidden. He blatantly disobeyed God's instruction to the family of Abraham, and God soon realized that this wasn't a man He could work with. Therefore, God had already left him, which was the result of his temporary lack of judgment in selling his birthright. I used the word "blatant" in my description of Esau's disobedience because if marrying the first Edomite woman was a mistake or an error, we can't say he made a mistake when he married the second Edomite woman.

As we witness churches being converted in large numbers into pubs, clubs, and mosques, alongside the shutting down of any conversation surrounding Christianity, there is also an uptick in the number of British people embracing the gods of the East.

Many Christians have adopted Hindu practices without giving it much thought. A significant number of English natives keep Buddha statues in their homes, with many embracing this trend, believing it brings them luck. Ironically, many of these individuals are quick to tell young Christians that they don't believe in anything. Yet, if they believe in connecting with their soul through yoga or that Buddha can bring them luck, they do, in fact, believe in something, just that they have overlooked the most important aspect, which is the Christian faith.

The UK is not an isolated case, as there are some concerning trends regarding online hostility toward Christianity in Nigeria. There is an increasing number of online warriors in Nigeria who seek every chance to undermine Christianity. Many of these individuals have reverted to worshiping idols, claiming they have returned to their original religion. The kind of rituals associated with idol worship can sometimes be very barbaric, which is a great concern for a Christian to return to. It's true that society can sometimes leave people feeling isolated or disconnected, making them more vulnerable. In times of hopelessness, people need hope, and it is only in Christ that we will find that hope. Unfortunately, the actions of these online warriors haven't helped, as our society doesn't provide the hope that individuals need during difficult times.

The West is in a very privileged position in God's agenda. It was not a mistake that the Judeo-Christian religion was established and became deeply rooted in the Global West. Even the founders of the United States of America established the nation on the Judeo-Christian faith. What we are witnessing currently is a pivot to the East. Sadly, each time people move to the East in the Bible, it was a walk away from God.

## Light in the Last Days

We see Western businesses leaving in droves and moving to the East. Moving to the East in itself is not supposed to be an issue, but dropping the Judeo-Christian faith and embracing the gods of the East runs contrary to the salvation through Christ, which we once believed. Interestingly, a lot of people in the East are turning to the West and embracing the God of the Bible, the Judeo-Christian faith.

A growing number of people in the United Kingdom have been voicing their frustration over the visible expression of Christian faith by many African migrants. However, what many of these critics fail to understand is the reality of the spiritual realm. For the sake of clarity, it's important to recognize that the nations which once received missionaries from the UK have now become the ones sending believers back, to spiritually support and help revive the UK.

This is the hand of God at work. He is ensuring that the message of the Gospel is not silenced in the United Kingdom. Many of these believers might think they are coming to the UK to study or work, pursuing their own goals, without realizing that God is actually sending them as missionaries, to help keep the Gospel alive.

Many migrants who came to the UK are simply going about their daily lives but soon came to a powerful realization that the Word of God must not be silenced in the very nation that once carried the Gospel across the world.

As they witnessed native churches closing down and being converted into mosques, temples, or even pubs, they felt a divine calling. Led by the Holy Spirit, these African believers began planting churches across the country, determined to keep the flame of the Christian faith burning bright in the UK.

This isn't just about Africans alone, brethren from Africa, the Caribbean, and from around the world are now joining hands in support of the remaining saints, natives of the United Kingdom, to guard the flames of Christianity and keep the torch burning.

God still has love for the United Kingdom, not just for the saints still holding the fort, but for the sake of the fathers of the faith who worked hard for the sake of the good news. It is still God's desire to return the United Kingdom to the path of prosperity.

# CHAPTER ELEVEN

## *God is waiting*

Sometimes we become weary and bogged down by the daily troubles of life, leading us to question the benefit of living for God. This can result in our desire to set ourselves free from Him, just to enjoy what seems like the freedom and alternatives outside of God. The prodigal son did the same, he looked down on the protection and comfort he once enjoyed from his father. He became more interested in the illusion of freedom and the alternatives outside his father's confines.

1 Peter 5:8 says, "Be sober-minded; be watchful. Your adversary the devil prowls around like a roaring lion, seeking someone to devour."

It's easy to be tempted into thinking that walking away from God costs nothing, especially when we see several billionaires who aren't Christians, particularly for those who associate success solely with wealth. But if riches were all we needed to fix everything, then many of the world's wealthiest wouldn't be struggling with depression or spending so much time in therapy.

Most of you reading this haven't suffered depression to the point of requiring extensive counseling sessions, which is, in itself, an indication of the relative peace you currently enjoy.

This brings to mind a quote by Dr. Sheri Jacobson, founder of Harley Therapy Ltd: "Grass is greener syndrome means that you have an inability to feel content with your life as it is, and relentlessly seek something better." She went on to say, "The temptation that the grass is greener on the other side is the idea that other people's lives are better than our own, and that we should be envious of what they have."

Clearly, the temptation to experience "what else is out there" or to enjoy what the world offers as an alternative to life under God can lead us to take a break from Him.

We all wrestle with questions about the world around us. The truth is, we only know in part, no one fully understands God. Even Moses, who saw God in part, did not know all of Him.

From waking up in the morning, rushing into a busy day, returning home in the evening, and sometimes staying awake at night pondering the meaning of life, it can often feel like a repetitive cycle: wake up, go to work, come home, sleep, and start all over the next day. In the process, we grow older, our hair turns grey, and we wonder if this is all there is to life. The rich, despite their wealth, long for immortality, hoping they could live forever to enjoy it, but they are unable to make that happen. Meanwhile, the poor question when their struggles will end, desperately hoping for a miracle. These thoughts lead many to conclude that life is meaningless, which can cause some to either contemplate ending it or live recklessly. However, those who view life as meaningless are often those who separate our earthly existence from the spiritual realm. Arguably, the events we experience in the physical world are ultimately shaped and influenced by forces or principles originating from a non-physical, spiritual realm. The truth is, we all have a purpose, one that is defined by our Creator. Every living person is created to worship God, and our lives exist at His pleasure. Even though God instructed Adam to tend the garden, He still came down in the cool of the evening to fellowship with him. The Bible places a significant emphasis on both "fellowship" and tending the garden, showing us that life is more than just labor, it is about relationship with God.

Matthew 6:10 says, "Your kingdom come, your will be done, on earth as it is in heaven." This expresses the desire for God's will to be made manifest on earth. Revelation 4:8 talks about the continuous worship "day and night" which signifies the eternal, unceasing nature of praise in heaven. If this is the picture of heaven, then to replicate it on earth means we were all created to worship God day and night.

For those of us who may have taken a break or walked away from God, it's important to remember: God never shuts the door. The truth remains, He loved us first, regardless of our current state. He loves us right now, just as we are. He's waiting for us, ready to step in if we let Him. He's waiting for us to bring that marriage issue, that health concern, that anxiety-causing situation to Him.

Christ's formula works. It may differ from what governments or society propose, but it brings the peace we're all searching for.

The devil once offered Jesus an alternative when he took Him to the top of the temple and mountain, but Jesus resisted (Matthew 4:1–11). Unfortunately, Adam and Eve gave in when the devil offered them an alternative to God. They didn't realize the deception, they saw freedom but didn't see the servitude hidden within it. Like the prodigal son, they saw a world of beauty and fun, but not the lack and slavery behind it.

Instead of making assumptions about God's supposed malevolence or looking for reasons to turn away, it is far better to focus on His love, as a Father. Many people who don't understand Jesus have never taken the time to listen to His teachings. The world is changing fast, and as Christians, we are not called to cocoon ourselves in a bubble of presumed safety.

The best time to focus more on God is when we feel most tempted to take a break from Him. In essence, the best time to pray is when we don't feel like praying. But how do we pray in difficult times? It starts with shutting out the noise and remaining consistent.

Moses pitched the tent of meeting outside the camp, he deliberately chose a place free from the noise and the hustle and bustle of Israel's camp. Similarly, Habakkuk sought solitude on a rooftop to seek God's face. These intentional acts of stepping away from distraction are what allow for intimacy with God.

The book of Habakkuk 2:1–2 is a true representation of what is expected of us during times of chaos, dissatisfaction, and the temptation to "give God a break"

- I will stand at my watch and station myself on the ramparts; I will look to see what he will say to me, and what answer I am to give to this complaint.

- Then the Lord replied: "Write down the revelation and make it plain on tablets so that a herald[b] may run with it.

Just as we are witnessing in our world today, many people feel a deep sense of disaffection about their life's purpose. Many Christians find themselves questioning whether God truly cares, wondering, "Where is God in the midst of all this chaos?" These are often genuine concerns. Some have fasted and prayed for their sick child. Others have put their faith in God, trusting that He would turn their difficult circumstances around.

The prophet Habakkuk brought his complaint to God. But instead of walking away after voicing his frustration, he chose to wait and listen for God's response and God answered him. Therefore, after we've prayed and asked God for help, we must also choose to stand and wait.

God does not ignore our concerns He cares deeply. When Thomas doubted the resurrection of Christ, his concerns were not dismissed. Christ came back specifically to address that doubt.

The reasons why God answers some prayers immediately and others seem to go unanswered can be difficult to understand. Sometimes, our difficulties may be the result of our own missteps. In other cases, it may simply not be the right time for God's response, or the reason for His silence is beyond our current understanding.

# CHAPTER-TWELVE

## *The Glory of God*

Stephen Fry is a well-known actor and self-proclaimed atheist who, in a popular interview, was asked: "What if, after death, it turns out that there is a God?"

Stephen Fry's response to what he would say to God in the afterlife was: "Bone cancer in children? How dare you!" He went on to describe God as capricious, mean-minded, and stupid for creating a world filled with injustice and pain.

Fry argued that the moment we banish God from human affairs, our lives would become simpler, purer, and cleaner. This view reflects the central position of many atheists, and even some who identify as agnostic. Unfortunately, pretending there is no God does not eliminate evil from the world, nor does Fry's perspective offer any real solution to the injustices we see today.

In truth, Stephen Fry's reaction to the question of why a loving God would allow evil, pain, and injustice is not unique. This is a question that burdens many, Christians and non-Christians alike. But our emotional responses should not translate into disrespect for God.

Human beings often overestimate their own intelligence and understanding, attempting to compare their limited wisdom with

God's, whose knowledge is infinite. Many live under the illusion that they are as wise as God, forgetting that true wisdom originates from Him. Holding such views doesn't make people look like wise men without clothes, it actually makes them look like naughty children without clothes.

When we place too much emphasis on our own intellect, we inevitably struggle to acknowledge God's superior knowledge and power. As a result, we find it difficult to truly submit to His wisdom.

Across the world, people humble themselves before their gods. Hindus bow before the cows they worship. Baal worshipers bowed before the statue of Baal. Muslims bow in reverence during prayer. Even heathens show submission to the deities they revere.

Now, consider someone who claims to be an atheist, professing not to believe in anything. I would like to point out that they still show reverence to their kings and queens. They stand in respect when the president or someone in authority enters the room.

So, the act of reverence and submission is not foreign to us, it's ingrained in human behavior and exists across cultures and beliefs.

Whether it's through religious rituals like bowing before gods or societal customs like kneeling before a monarch, these acts of reverence seem to acknowledge something beyond one's personal sense of self or power.

In many ways, such gestures can be seen as a recognition of a higher authority, whether that authority is a god, a ruler, or even an idea that commands respect. When people kneel before kings, gods, or symbols of authority, they appear to acknowledge that there is something, or someone greater than themselves.

Even atheists, or those who don't subscribe to a particular religious belief, still engage in moments of submission or reverence. These acts, whether consciously recognized or not, still carry meaning. It's fascinating how rituals and behaviors can symbolize a deeper acknowledgment of something greater than the individual.

If all this is true, then why do we sometimes view complete submission to the will of the All-Powerful, Most Sovereign God as excessive?

Interestingly, our view of God greatly influences how we relate to Him. If we perceive God as small or insignificant, we're likely to treat Him casually and without due regard. But if we truly see Him as the Almighty, we will approach Him with reverence and awe.

Apart from the moment when Solomon sacrificed to God and the glory of God descended in the temple, in 2 Chronicles 7, let's consider how the children of Israel perceived God when they came before Him.

Exodus 19:9- 20 [NIV]. The Lord said to Moses, "I am going to come to you in a dense cloud, so that the people will hear me speaking with you and will always put their trust in you." Then Moses told the Lord what the people had said.

10 And the Lord said to Moses, "Go to the people and consecrate them today and tomorrow. Have them wash their clothes 11 and be ready by the third day, because on that day the Lord will come down on Mount Sinai in the sight of all the people. 12 Put limits for the people around the mountain and tell them, 'Be careful that you do not approach the mountain or touch the foot of it. Whoever touches the mountain is to be put to death. 13 They are to be stoned or shot with arrows; not a hand is to be laid on them. No person or animal shall be permitted to live.' Only when the ram's horn sounds a long blast may they approach the mountain. 14 After Moses had gone down the mountain to the people, he consecrated them, and they washed their clothes. 15 Then he said to the people, "Prepare yourselves for the third day. Abstain from sexual relations. 16 On the morning of the third day there was thunder and lightning, with a thick cloud over the mountain, and a very loud trumpet blast. Everyone in the camp trembled. 17 Then Moses led the people out of the camp to meet

with God, and they stood at the foot of the mountain. 18 Mount Sinai was covered with smoke, because the Lord descended on it in fire. The smoke billowed up from it like smoke from a furnace, and the whole mountain[b] trembled violently. 19 As the sound of the trumpet grew louder and louder, Moses spoke and the voice of God answered him.[c]

20 The Lord descended to the top of Mount Sinai and called Moses to the top of the mountain. So Moses went up 21 and the Lord said to him, "Go down and warn the people so they do not force their way through to see the Lord and many of them perish. 22 Even the priests, who approach the Lord, must consecrate themselves, or the Lord will break out against them."

Exodus 20: 18-19 [NIV]. 18 "When the people saw the thunder and lightning and heard the trumpet and saw the mountain in smoke, they trembled with fear. They stayed at a distance 19 and said to Moses, "Speak to us yourself and we will listen. But do not have God speak to us or we will die."

Arguably, if Stephen Fry were to stand before God, the glory of God would be too overwhelming for him to question Him. There are several examples in the Bible where people encountered the glory of God, and these moments show just how small and insignificant man can feel in the presence of God's almightiness.

- Prophet Isaiah.

Isaiah 6:1-7 [NIV]. "1 In the year that king Uzziah died I saw also the Lord sitting upon a throne, high and lifted up, and his train filled the temple. 2 Above it stood the seraphims: each one had six wings; with twain he covered his face, and with twain he covered his feet, and with twain he did fly. 3 And one cried unto another, and said, Holy, holy, holy, is the Lord of hosts: the whole earth is full of his glory. 4 And the posts of the door moved at the voice of him that cried, and the house was filled with smoke. 5 Then said I, Woe is me! for I am undone; because I am a man of unclean lips, and I dwell in the midst of a people of unclean lips: for mine eyes have seen the King, the Lord of hosts. 6 Then flew one of the seraphims unto me, having a live coal in his hand, which he had taken with the tongs from off the altar: 7 And he laid it upon my mouth, and said, Lo, this hath touched thy lips; and thine iniquity is taken away, and thy sin purged."

- Moses by the burning bush

Exodus 3:5 -6. "5 And he said, Draw not nigh hither: put off thy shoes from off thy feet, for the place whereon thou standest is holy ground. 6 Moreover he said, I am the God of thy father, the God of Abraham, the God of Isaac, and the God of Jacob. And Moses hid his face; for he was afraid to look upon God."

Moses came before the burning bush and without being asked to do so, he bowed his head.

- Saul on his way to Damascus.

Acts 9 1-5 (NKJV). "1Then Saul, still breathing threats and murder against the disciples of the Lord, went to the high priest 2 and asked letters from him to the synagogues of Damascus, so that if he found any who were of the Way, whether men or women, he might bring them bound to Jerusalem. 3 As he journeyed, he came near Damascus, and suddenly a light shone around him from heaven. 4 Then he fell to the ground, and heard a voice saying to him, "Saul, Saul, why are you persecuting Me? 5 And he said, "Who are You, Lord?" Then the Lord said, "I am Jesus, whom you are persecuting. ]It is hard for you to kick against the goads."

When Saul encountered Jesus on his road to Damascus experience, he suddenly lay face down, and referred to Jesus as Lord.

*Light in the Last Days*

- Peter's life changing experience after a big catch of fish.

Luke 5 :4 -11 [NIV]. "4 When he had finished speaking, he said to Simon, "Put out into deep water, and let down the nets for a catch. 5 Simon answered, "Master, we've worked hard all night and haven't caught anything. But because you say so, I will let down the nets. 6 When they had done so, they caught such a large number of fish that their nets began to break. 7 So they signalled their partners in the other boat to come and help them, and they came and filled both boats so full that they began to sink. 8 When Simon Peter saw this, he fell at Jesus' knees and said, "Go away from me, Lord; I am a sinful man!" 9 For he and all his companions were astonished at the catch of fish they had taken, 10 and so were James and John, the sons of Zebedee, Simon's partners. Then Jesus said to Simon, "Don't be afraid; from now on you will fish for people." 11 So they pulled their boats up on shore, left everything and followed him."

Simon Peter initially referred to Jesus as Master and spoke with Him in a casual, conversational manner before Jesus encouraged him to cast his net for a catch. However, after the miraculous catch, Peter referred to Jesus as Lord. His perception of Christ changed dramatically following the net-breaking fishing experience. Suddenly, he saw Jesus through a different lens and recognized His divinity, so much so that he described himself as a sinner who was unworthy to be in the presence of God.

- John the beloved.

Revelation 1: 12- 17. ESV. "12 I turned around to see the voice that was speaking to me. And when I turned I saw seven golden lampstands, 13 and among the lampstands was someone like a son of man, [d] dressed in a robe reaching down to his feet and with a golden sash around his chest. 14 The hair on his head was white like wool, as white as snow, and his eyes were like blazing fire. 15

His feet were like bronze glowing in a furnace, and his voice was like the sound of rushing waters. 16 In his right hand he held seven stars, and coming out of his mouth was a sharp, double-edged sword. His face was like the sun shining in all its brilliance. 17 When I saw him, I fell at his feet as though dead. Then he placed his right hand on me and said: "Do not be afraid. I am the First and the Last. 18 I am the Living One; I was dead, and now look, I am alive for ever and ever! And I hold the keys of death and Hades."

We all know how close Jesus was with John the Beloved. He was known as the disciple who was always by Jesus's side. Even as Jesus took His last breath, He entrusted John with the care of His mother, Mary, a gesture that highlights the deep bond between them. Interestingly, when John the Beloved later saw the same Jesus in His full glory, he could not even look at Him. Instead, he fell facedown in awe and reverence.

The glory of God is so powerful that when we come into His presence, we are overwhelmed. In that moment, we realize just how small we truly are. Whatever importance or value we may have placed on ourselves is immediately reduced in the face of the Almighty.

God Himself does not strip us of our value or intellect, but the sheer magnitude of His glory humbles us. In truth, God loves us deeply, and our true worth comes from Him, not from what we think of ourselves, nor from how much we believe we know.

- Let's consider the story of the woman caught in adultery

In the book of John, chapter 8, a woman was brought before Jesus by a group of men who were seeking His opinion on the appropriate punishment for her. Their intention was to trap Jesus, but they forgot that God is all-knowing.

## Light in the Last Days

When Jesus said, "Let anyone of you who is without sin be the first to throw a stone at her," the Bible tells us that they left one by one, until no one remained.

These men weren't doing anything unusual, they were simply following what their custom and the Law of Moses required. But this moment stands as a powerful example of the law coming face to face with righteousness. While the men were projecting the law, Christ was demonstrating forgiveness as the true path to righteousness. What's interesting about this story is that none of the men argued with Jesus. None tried to justify their moral right to punish the woman. No one said, "My sin isn't as bad as hers." This is a clear picture of what happens when we truly come before God.

If these hardened men were unable to rationalize their actions in front of Christ, while He was in human form, then how can we expect to justify our moral views and choices when we stand before the judgment throne of God?

Not one of them dared to cast a stone to enforce the Law of Moses, because there was enough sin to go around. And just like that, their desire to see the woman punished melted away like mist on a hot summer day.

- The Israelites in the wilderness, Exodus 34:29-35.

The Israelites could not even look at Moses after he had spent time with God. If this was the effect of merely being in God's presence, how then could we possibly behold God Himself?

Some might ask, "If the glory of God is so overwhelming, how were the Pharisees able to confront Christ?" The truth is, Christ was measured, He intentionally withheld the fullness of His glory from those who did not believe. He spoke of Himself, but often in ways that were subtle or veiled, so that only those who were truly thirsty would seek and find the truth.

I have never experienced a tsunami firsthand, and I think it's better to watch the sheer force of one on camera than to be standing on the shore when it strikes. Those who have faced the might of a tsunami up close know how terrifying and overwhelming it can be.

In the same way, we might consider the overwhelming glory of the sun, it's impossible to approach or even stare at the sun directly. Now imagine the God behind that force of nature.

Arguably, God loves us so deeply that, just as earthly children sometimes express their frustrations and question their parents' decisions, God has made room for us to do the same with Him. His love allows space for our questions, even in our moments of doubt.

Luke 10:40-41 [NIV]. "40 But Martha was distracted by all the preparations that had to be made. She came to him and asked, "Lord, don't you care that my sister has left me to do the work by myself? Tell her to help me!" 41 "Martha, Martha," the Lord answered, "you are worried and upset about many things, 42 but few things are needed—or indeed only one.[a] Mary has chosen what is better, and it will not be taken away from her."

In verse 40 above, if we put Martha's comments into context, we can conclude that Martha was kind of telling Jesus off, for not asking her sister to give her a helping hand. Despite her outburst, we will notice that Martha did not talk back to Jesus after He admonished her, that was where the reverence comes in.

Luke 15:28-32 [NIV]. 28 "The older brother became angry and refused to go in. So his father went out and pleaded with him. 29 But he answered his father, 'Look! All these years I've been slaving for you and never disobeyed your orders. Yet you never gave me even a young goat so I could celebrate with my friends. 30 But when this son of yours who has squandered your property with prostitutes comes home, you kill the fattened calf for him!'

31 "'My son,' the father said, 'you are always with me, and everything I have is yours. 32 But we had to celebrate and be glad, because this brother of yours was dead and is alive again; he was lost and is found.'"

Take a look at the story of the prodigal son, and how the eldest son felt betrayed by his father for throwing a party to celebrate the return of his wayward brother. The father didn't lash out or respond with anger toward the older son for how he felt. Instead, he gently explained the situation to him, just as Jesus did with Martha.

The father in this parable represents God and His relationship with us. God's love gives us the space to express how we feel, but it must always be done with reverence.

Another example is the story of Thomas, who doubted the resurrection of Jesus. Jesus returned specifically to address Thomas's doubt. He didn't scold or rebuke him harshly. Instead, He gently admonished Thomas, saying, "Blessed are those who believe without seeing."

John 20:24-29

24. Now Thomas (also known as Didymus[a]), one of the Twelve, was not with the disciples when Jesus came. 25 So the other disciples told him, "We have seen the Lord!"

But he said to them, "Unless I see the nail marks in his hands and put my finger where the nails were, and put my hand into his side, I will not believe."

26 A week later his disciples were in the house again, and Thomas was with them. Though the doors were locked, Jesus came and stood among them and said, "Peace be with you!" 27 Then he said to Thomas, "Put your finger here; see my hands. Reach out your hand and put it into my side. Stop doubting and believe."

28 Thomas said to him, "My Lord and my God!"

29 Then Jesus told him, "Because you have seen me, you have believed; blessed are those who have not seen and yet have believed."

The way Jesus handled Thomas's disbelief wasn't with the kind of show of force we might expect between a master and a servant, but rather with a brotherly kind of love and this is God's style.

There are other examples in Scripture that help shed more light on this, offering meaningful comparisons.

Elijah, for instance, walked for forty days and forty nights to reach Mount Horeb (also known as Mount Sinai) after fleeing from Jezebel. Though he was running away from Jezebel, he was actually running toward God just to have a conversation with Him. When Elijah finally arrived, he encountered God, because he knew with certainty that God would not be unavoidably absent after such an exhausting, purposeful journey.

When David felt frustrated that Saul was pursuing him, he didn't turn his back on God in the midst of his battles. Instead, he continually called on God to come to his rescue.

In 1 Samuel 24:4–13, we see how God placed King Saul at David's mercy, demonstrating to David that God had been with him all along and had his back the entire time.

Also, when Joshua experienced defeat in battle against the men of Ai, he went to God and asked why He had allowed them to be defeated. In all the examples above, the people involved felt some level of frustration with God and were, in a way, complaining to Him about their difficulties.

The key difference between these cases and the murmuring of the Israelites in the wilderness which angered God, was their attitude. The Israelites saw God as incapable of helping them. They cried out that He had brought them into the wilderness only to kill them, and even said they would rather return to Egypt.

Elijah, David, and Joshua, on the other hand, ran to God with their frustrations, and God gave each of them a listening ear. It is okay to cry out to God, and it is okay to ask, "Lord, why are all these things happening to me?"

Our final example is that of Jonah and his reluctance to see the people of Nineveh reconciled with God. Even after God used a great fish to bring Jonah to Nineveh, he still struggled with God and begrudgingly delivered the message. Jonah felt offended by God's mercy, as shown in their back-and-forth conversation. Yet, we see how far God went to appeal to Jonah's conscience and help him understand His compassion.

The idea that an all-powerful, all-knowing, and loving God would allow evil and injustice in the world is something humans have always found difficult to reconcile.

I once sat in a congregation and listened to Jonathan Tremaine Thomas talk about his past struggles as a young Black man, questioning why a loving God would allow slavery as he imagined the horrors his ancestors suffered at the hands of their slave masters. Consequently, Stephen Fry's view is not an isolated case, but the idea of God as malevolent or an angry father is far from the truth.

Even Christians themselves are sometimes burdened with questions as they, their loved ones, or friends suffer from natural disasters, illnesses like cancer, brain tumors, and other degenerative diseases. The truth is that people are hurting, and even devoted Christians aren't spared, they are also hurting and seeking answers to the many questions in their minds about the world they live in.

Just like Stephen Fry, atheists often point to the problems in the world and blame God for allowing them to happen. But the truth is that atheism does not remove the pain and suffering in the world. What it does is remove all hope.

John Lennox seems to offer a more brilliant perspective when he uses the analogy of beauty and barbed wire to describe the mixed world we live in: a beautiful world with too many troubles in it.

At the center of Christianity is the cross, and it is here that God and human suffering meet. God did not separate Himself from our suffering; rather, He is at the center of it. He is at the center of the cross, where He bore all our suffering.

What makes Christianity distinctive is that you must believe in order to experience it. John Lennox emphasized that at the heart of Christianity is a different kind of sacrifice, one that focuses on God's sacrifice. Our sacrifice is important, as the Bible encourages us to offer ourselves as a living sacrifice. The key sacrifice for a Christian is simply to believe in God wholeheartedly. The truth remains that it is God's sacrifice that empowers us to make sacrifices on our part.

Jordan Peterson's analogy seems to draw a parallel to why God's idea of free will is essential in the affairs of men. He pointed out that a mother's sacrifice for her infant child is an incredibly selfless act, often putting the mother second. However, he also expanded his analogy by saying that a mother might become overprotective and attempt to shield her child from the suffering of the world. Ultimately, this could turn her into a "devouring mother," as such an act would prevent the child from thriving. This illustrates that having God by our side does not mean the absence of troubles. What matters is that, with God beside you, the troubles won't overwhelm you. God will not shield you from life's challenges, especially if He has a purpose for your life, because these challenges are meant to shape you into maturity. Consider David, Joseph, Moses, Gideon, Deborah, and many others, it was through the trials they faced that God shaped them.

The wedding at Cana of Galilee ran out of wine but the situation did not get out of hand because Christ was there. The storm came as the disciples were crossing the sea of Galilee, but the boat did not sink because Jesus was in the boat. These examples do nothing but give us hope in difficult times, because that hope is the force that helps us to fight on.

Yes, there are sufferings in the world and yes, there are injustices in the world, but God is saying you still need me.

I will liken this to a mum whose family is being attacked by marauders. She immediately reached for her phone and called for help from the police after her earlier screams for help from neighbours were unanswered.

She then saw the attackers approaching her direction and as they drew closer to where she and her four kids were hiding, confused on why the police weren't there to help, she decided to fight off the attackers.

Unfortunately, they struck and killed one of her children, she then made a run with her remaining three kids and hid somewhere.

She picked up the phone again and started calling the police asking them to make haste, whilst screaming through the window to neighbours to come to her rescue.

The attackers remained in the premises, in search of this mother and her kids as they are keen to finish them off, but moments later neighbours rushed in to help and the police eventually arrived at the scene and the marauders were arrested.

This mother will remain unhappy that the neighbours and the police did not come to their rescue on time, because if they had responded promptly, she would not have lost one of her children. However, despite her dissatisfaction with the neighbours and the police, she realised she still needed them to keep her and the rest of her kids safe from the marauders.

This is our situation with God, despite our dissatisfaction over the fact that our prayers to God to heal our loved ones and take away our hardships were not answered, this does not mean we no longer need God to keep our living relatives safe and in good health.

Just like the attackers who remained after killing one of this woman's four children, the sickness that took the life of our loved ones is still out there. There are still murderers and rapists, and there are still raging wars for those in the war zones. Therefore, we still need God to be there for the living.

Consequently, the fact that our specific prayers were not answered or our expectations not met does not mean we no longer need God in other areas of our lives.

God is interested in the minutiae of things that concern us. He's keen to address our worries and unhappiness. However, God is not eager to display His overwhelming glory when He relates with us because He knows it would be too much for us. He prefers a cordial atmosphere.

The manner in which God spoke to Cain about his anger, after Cain was upset that God rejected his offering, was quite cordial. More so, imagine how the father of the prodigal son approached his eldest son when he realized he was unhappy and refused to come into the house to be a part of the banquet.

The father went to him to address his concerns. In like manner, for those of you who are hurting, I am certain God is speaking to you right now about those concerns of yours. He is saying He still cares, but you need to be still to hear what He's saying to you.

I would conclude this chapter by focusing on what I believe God places ahead of healing and everything else in His dealings with us, and that is **SALVATION.**

The story in the book of Luke 5:5:18-25 [NIV]. shines some light on this: "18 Some men came carrying a paralyzed man on a mat and tried to take him into the house to lay him before Jesus. 19 When they could not find a way to do this because of the crowd, they went up on the roof and lowered him on his mat through the tiles into the middle of the crowd, right in front of Jesus. 20 When Jesus saw their faith, he said, "Friend, your sins are forgiven." 21 The Pharisees and the teachers of the law began thinking to themselves, "Who is this fellow who speaks blasphemy? Who can forgive sins but God alone?" 22 Jesus knew what they were thinking and asked, "Why are you thinking these things in your hearts? 23 Which is easier: to say, 'Your sins are forgiven,' or to say, 'Get up and walk'? 24 But I want you to know that the Son of Man has authority on earth to forgive sins." So he said to the paralyzed man, "I tell you, get up, take your mat and go home." 25 Immediately he stood up in front of them, took what he had been lying on and went home praising God."

Christ offered forgiveness of sin to this sick man first because Christ knew that every man needed salvation more than healing. This does not diminish the need for healing, but the body we need healing for is only for our temporal stay here on earth, while salvation is for eternity.

Let's be reminded of the value God places on every soul. The soul of any man is worth more than all the assets on earth put together. The Bible says, "What shall it profit a man to gain the whole world and lose his soul?" The Bible also asks, "What can a man exchange for his soul?" This question means there is nothing you have, your billions of pounds, your trillions of dollars, or your position as president, that is worth enough to exchange for a soul.

The soul is the defining feature that sets humans apart from all other creations of God, allowing them to have a spiritual dimension and moral authority, which other animals lack. God created humans in His own image and breathed into them. He gave them a soul, which is considered the essence of life and what sets humans apart as beings capable of advanced thought and spiritual connection with God.

Returning to the question of why Christ prioritized salvation over healing, the parable of the kingdom of heaven offers deeper insight into this.

Matthew 13:44-46 [NIV] 44 "The kingdom of heaven is like treasure hidden in a field. When a man found it, he hid it again, and then in his joy went and sold all he had and bought that field.

45 "Again, the kingdom of heaven is like a merchant looking for fine pearls. 46 When he found one of great value, he went away and sold everything he had and bought it.

The parables in Matthew 13:44–46 further emphasize the immense value of our salvation. Jesus illustrates that the Kingdom of Heaven is worth everything we possess. In the parable, the man sells all he has to purchase the hidden treasure, highlighting the word "everything." This implies total surrender; he was left with nothing else because he gave up all he owned just to obtain the treasure. In the context of our lives today, "everything" could represent sacrifices such as our car, job, possessions, family, and more, combined.

It's crucial to understand that even after you've given up everything for the sake of this treasure, your salvation, you must remain vigilant and spiritually alert. Please, do not fall into the trap of thinking, *"I've given my all, so there's nothing more I need to do."*

In Matthew 13:24 (NKJV), Jesus shares a parable that reminds us of how the enemy operates, sowing weeds among the wheat while men sleep. This illustrates the need to stay watchful. The relationship you have with Christ is a treasure, and it's your responsibility to guard it diligently. The devil will not sit idly by; he will continually try to draw you away from Christ. That's why you must protect your faith with intention and persistence.

# CHAPTER THIRTEEN

*God won't prove Himself to you in a Challenge.*

In recent years, many people have increasingly requested that God prove His existence or Himself. I sometimes watch with amusement when people say, "God, if You are real and exist, strike me," and when they don't get any response, they say, "I tell you, God doesn't exist, because if He is real, as the Bible claims, then He should have struck me."

Rarely do we hear or read that God forcefully proved Himself to people who do not believe in Him, except in a few cases such as when God forcefully demonstrated His might to Pharaoh through Moses.

There are other instances where people think in their hearts that they are genuinely working for God but are doing it the wrong way. One such example is when God proved His existence to Moses through the burning bush. This occurred because Moses, on his own initiative, wanted to rescue the children of Israel from the hands of the Egyptians, but he went about it in the wrong way. Saul, on the other hand, went to the judge to seek permission to prosecute God's enemies, accusing them of blasphemy against

God, until God encountered him and made him understand that the people he was persecuting were actually the ones doing good.

Just like God, Christ being a reflection of God never attempted to prove Himself or His abilities whenever He was confronted with such demands.

Christ spoke in parables and showed little concern about whether the multitudes He was preaching to understood or not. Yet, He waited to explain Himself in much clearer terms only to those who sought answers to the parables. This means that Christ was not concerned with the multitude but was instead focused on those who genuinely sought to know and understand God (or Him) more deeply.

(Mathew 4:3, And when the tempter came to Him, he said, if thou be the Son of God, command that these stones be made bread. [4:4] But He answered and said, it is written, man shall not live by bread alone, but by every word that proceed out of the mouth of God).

Christ didn't prove to the Devil He could change stones to bread, when He was tempted by the Devil even though His miracles proved He could.

(John 8:57-59, Then the Jews said to Him, "You are not yet fifty years old, and have You seen Abraham?" Jesus said to them, "Most assuredly, I say to you, before Abraham was, I AM." Then they took up stones to throw at Him; but Jesus hid Himself and went out of the temple, going through the midst of them and so passed by).

Christ did not justify further His claims of being around before Abraham was born.

(John 2:19-20, Jesus answered them, "Destroy this temple, and in three days I will raise it up." The Jews then said, "it took forty-six years to build this temple, and will You raise it in three days?")

Christ did not justify His comment of pulling down the temple and rebuilding it within three days, He didn't clarify the context of His statement.

(Luke 7: 22, Then Jesus answering said unto them, "Go your way, and tell John what things ye have seen and heard: how the blind see, the lame walk, the lepers are cleansed, the deaf hear, the dead are raised, to the poor the Gospel is preached).

Christ did not prove Himself to John the Baptist as the messiah, all He did was to refer John's disciples to the salvation of souls and the miracles He did.

(Matt 6: 2-3, 2 The next Sabbath, he began teaching in the synagogue, and many who heard him were astonished. They asked, "Where did he get all His wisdom and the power to perform such miracles? 3 He's just the carpenter, the son of Mary and brother of James, Joseph, Judas, and Simon and his sisters lives right here among us, they were deeply offended and refused to believe in him")

The pertinent question here remains, Why did the people of Nazareth bring their sick before Christ for healing, even when they didn't believe in Him? The only reason behind this act was to challenge Christ to prove Himself. The move was not about a genuine need for healing. However, Christ never made any extra effort to prove Himself, even when pressed by the unbelieving crowd. He couldn't, because the people did not have the faith to bring about a miracle; they weren't really interested in the miracle itself. They just wanted Christ to prove Himself, and that is why their sickness didn't get healed.

Just as the father of the prodigal son did not justify his authority over his son by insisting that he remain under his control, he gave his son what he requested and allowed him to make his own decision about whether to stay or go.

The parable of the prodigal son and the parable of the lost sheep share a great deal of similarity in terms of our relationship with God. Even though the lost sheep was not reported to have deliberately left the fold, what matters is that both the sheep and the prodigal son left the care of their guardians. The emphasis in both stories is the joy of the guardian and the celebration that followed when they returned home. It doesn't matter how far we've gone from God, nor does it matter how many millions or billions of people are already under God's care. All that matters is that He cares about you and is looking forward to your return. There is joy in heaven the moment we return to God.

God has demonstrated His ability to use even the smallest of people to do remarkably great things. He uses people who, by the world's standards, are considered unqualified to do mighty things, just to prove His might. He picked David among his brothers, even when he didn't look like it. He picked Gideon when he was the least among his people. There are several examples in the Bible and even in today's world where God picks people from nothing and makes them something, but we obviously cannot see what God is doing from the seat of unbelief.

Most of the world's greatest and celebrated scientists used God as their anchor. From George Washington, the founding father of the United States, to famous scientists such as Francis Bacon, Nicolaus Copernicus, Johannes Kepler, Galileo Galilei, Isaac Newton, Robert Boyle, Antoine Lavoisier, Thomas Edison, and Carl Friedrich Gauss, all are a testament to this. As you read this, I want you to know that God does not write anyone off because He sees greatness in all of us. God's hands are stretched out, and He is hoping you will take His hand in total surrender, so He can reveal Himself to you.

Several eyewitness stories have been told about God's divine hand on George Washington. One such vivid example is the story of "Bulletproof George Washington," where God proved His divine hand on George Washington. Among other examples, God used dew to keep George Washington from defeat at the hands of the enemy. Many today, for the sake of political correctness, describe these events surrounding George Washington as mere coincidences. God is a Father who makes something out of nothing. He uses the weak to achieve mighty things, just to shame the mighty. He used little David to defeat mighty Goliath. He used old water pots, seemingly forgotten, to make new wine with a taste that was too good to be true.

If Thomas had walked away saying he wouldn't believe Christ had resurrected until he thrust his finger through the prints in His hands and His side, Jesus Christ would not have come back to him to prove His resurrection. Despite Thomas's doubt, he stayed with the apostles in a locked room praying, and then Jesus showed up.

Dr. Frank Morison, a British lawyer and engineer, initially set out to write a book debunking the resurrection of Christ. However, as he delved into the evidence, something unexpected happened. The deeper he investigated, the more compelling he found the case for the resurrection. This once-skeptical lawyer became convinced by the facts and ultimately embraced the Christian faith. The result was not the book he had planned to write, but rather the now-famous "Who Moved the Stone?".

Morison approached his research with an open mind, genuinely seeking the truth. Although he started with doubts about the story of Christ, he didn't cling to his skepticism, he remained open to wherever the evidence might lead. In doing so, he brought to life the biblical principle: "Those who seek will find." And in his search, he found God.

During his Easter sermon, Pastor Tony Wastall shared a story about his father, who, after extensive travels in the East, developed an interest in Eastern religions and came to view all faiths as essentially the same, seeing nothing uniquely compelling about Christianity. However, everything changed when he read "Who Moved the Stone," the powerful book by Dr. Frank Morison. That book played a pivotal role in leading his father to embrace the Christian faith.

To this day, Dr. Frank Morison, a man who once set out to disprove the story of Christ, much like the Apostle Paul, continues to impact lives long after his passing. If you still have doubts about Christ, I encourage you to seek the truth with an open heart. I believe Christ will reveal Himself to you. And who knows? In the days to come, countless testimonies of salvation, redemption, and deliverance through Christ could be traced back to your journey of faith.

Let's consider this story. Patrick Bet-David is an American businessman, famous podcaster, author, and motivational speaker. He is known for founding PHP Agency. He stated that for 25 years, he was an atheist, saying, "I don't believe in God, I don't read the Bible, zero church, zero anything."

One day, after breaking up with his girlfriend, he was down and alone. Thirty minutes later, for no apparent reason, he felt the need to pray. He said, "My prayer started like this: God, I don't believe in You. I think it's fake. I think it's for weak people, but if You are out there, great. I want to know something, but if not, I am talking anyway. God, I haven't spoken to my mom for five years, but if You exist, I would love to talk to my mom." He said, "Thirty seconds later, I got a call from a blocked number, and it was my mom crying. I said, 'Why are you crying?' She said, 'I got the feeling you are in pain.

I asked, how did you get this number, she says, you know, I just got it six months ago. I don't know how to talk to her.' I hung up the phone. I sat in that car that night, chills all over my body. I'm like, 'Oh my God. Either this is ironic, or this is real, but the level of coincidence is a little too real. I could have chosen to say it's ironic, but I chose to believe it was God, and He has my back.'"

Just like Thomas in the Bible, who doubted Jesus' resurrection yet stayed in the upper room with the disciples praying, Patrick

Bet-David may not have believed in God, but he exercised faith by praying to Him anyway. If you say there is no God and then walk away, you will receive nothing.

The prodigal son had his 'come to Jesus' moment and he knew it. In that moment, he turned back to his father. Have you reached your own 'come to Jesus' moment without even realizing it? And if you do know you've hit that point, where your own wisdom has failed to fix the situation, what's still holding you back from coming to Jesus?

The Bible says that God is mindful of you, He knows your name, and He is thinking about you. These are not just mere words, they are real.

You may be in one corner of a room, in a remote area of the world, thinking that God has forgotten you. Or you might be in a busy, bustling city, wondering how God could possibly remember your needs among so many people. The world's population is about 8 billion, yet that did not stop God from remembering and responding to Patrick Bet-David's prayer within thirty minutes.

Interestingly, Patrick Bet-David wasn't a believer when he made this prayer, yet God answered him. Your case is not an isolated one. You might be thinking, "I don't know God, and I don't think He would answer me." My suggestion to you is this—just call on God and trust in Him for a response. The difference is that, since his encounter with God, Patrick Bet-David has drawn closer to Him. He built a relationship with God and now preaches His word. He did not stop at saying, "After all, God answered my prayer while I wasn't a Christian, so I will remain that way." The truth is that God reveals Himself to us to draw us closer to Him.

Jesus Christ responded to all who called out to Him, either for help or to seek answers to burning questions troubling their hearts. The rich young ruler went to Him and received a response. Nicodemus went to Him at night and received an answer. Even when Blind Bartimaeus screamed out for help, he also received a response.

The common feature here is that all these people were humble and genuine in their quest for answers.

God did not prove to Adam and Eve what fate would befall them if they disobeyed; all God did was give them His instructions. In the same way, God has issued His instructions to us. Whether we choose to listen or not is a decision we must make.

Unfortunately, the limitations of human wisdom mean that things of God will always remain foolish to those who see themselves as wise. Just like Lord Nelson, who fought the Battle of Trafalgar, George Washington knew the God he served, which informed the reason he founded the United States of America on God.

As you read this, I want you to know that God does not write anyone off because He sees greatness in all of us. God's hands are stretched out, and He is hoping you will take His hand in total surrender, and then He will reveal Himself to you.

God is still in the business of proving Himself. Many Christians and non-Christians alike have testified to how God proved and revealed Himself to them in their quest for answers. But in all these cases, these people will confirm to you that these revelations come about through days of prayer, a seeking heart, and humility.

God does not force anyone to love Him, His terms are simple: "If you want to spend your life after death with Him in heaven, then do His will on earth. But if you want to do your will on earth, then you will spend your life after death somewhere else." This is all about choice. When the prodigal son wanted to do his own thing, the father didn't force him to do otherwise. God is willing to prove Himself, but only to those who seek answers genuinely and humbly. At death, when our opportunity to repent is no more, it wouldn't be good to find out if our gamble of requesting God to prove Himself before we believe in Him was a good one or not.

# CHAPTER FOURTEEN

## *The mystery of the spirit realm*

The realm of the spirit is guided by principles, it doesn't matter if it is God or the devil. These principles are an active force that provokes reactions.

- Utterances
- Blood Sacrifices
- Boundaries

As far as the spirit realm is concerned, utterances are words, decrees, enchantments, or invocations made by one person over another, with the intention of achieving a specific outcome. On the other hand, utterances can also involve accepting certain pronouncements and decrees upon ourselves, whether promises or curses. Words are an active force, a vehicle that carries both life and death.

In Genesis 1:1-3, the bible said the holy spirit brooded over the waters, but nothing happened until the word came forth, that is the power of spoken word. With our words we can define our destiny, make and break things.

The Bible book of Proverbs 18:21 tells us of the power of the tongue. Balak expected Balaam to curse the Israelites which is one example of the power of utterance (Numbers 22). Balak would not have engaged Balaam, the non-Jewish sorcerer and prophet, to curse the Israelites if he didn't believe there was power in the tongue. God Himself knew the power of Balaam's words, that's why He did not allow Balaam to utter the curses he was hired to speak.

Consider God's promise to Abraham, which He had to swear by His own name. There are other examples of utterances, such as the pronouncements made by a father over his children. Take, for example, the story of Noah—his drunkenness, his son's poor judgment, and the resulting consequences.

Genesis 9:24-27 [NIV]. "24 When Noah sobered up, he found out what his youngest son had done to him. 25 So he said, "Canaan is cursed! He will be the lowest slave to his brothers. 26 Praise the Lord, the God of Shem! Canaan will be his slave. 27 May God expands the territory of Japheth.[a] May he live in the tents of Shem. Canaan will be his slave."

In our world today, we are quick to say that respect must be earned and this is absolutely true. But as far as the spirit realm is concerned, parents have a God-given authority over their children. Children who are estranged from their parents often live with a certain void. No matter their wealth, their happiness is never truly complete, no matter how well they mask it. The curse on Reuben from his father, Jacob, adds another dimension to the power of utterances.

Genesis 49:3-4 [NIV]. 3."Reuben, you are my firstborn, my strength, the very first son I had, first in majesty and first in power. 4 You will no longer be first because you were out of control like a flood and you climbed into your father's bed. Then you dishonored it. He climbed up on my couch."

Unfortunately, Jacob's curse plagued the descendants of Reuben up until the days of Moses. Before his death, Moses undertook the fundamental task of reversing this curse, which had held the tribe of Reuben down for nearly 400 years.

Deuteronomy 33:6 [NIV]. "May the tribe of Reuben live and not die out, though their people are few in number."

This is also an indication that, just like Moses, an ordained man of God can break generational curses over our lives. However, there is no need to stir up a hornet's nest with one's parents while hoping that an ordained man of God in your church will reverse whatever pronouncements they have made concerning your life. Reversing parental pronouncements is not easy, and in most cases, some irreparable damage may have already been done before these curses are lifted.

Let's consider this subject in the context of a child who has been wronged. Ishmael was about 14 years old when Isaac was born, as Abraham was 86 when Ishmael was born and 100 when Isaac arrived. While the exact age of Isaac at the time of his weaning isn't known, it is assumed that Ishmael was likely between 17 and 19 years old when he and his mother were sent away. This means Ishmael was old enough to understand the trauma of their rejection. It wasn't a story told to him, it was a painful experience he lived through personally, one that would stay with him for life.

Reflecting on this, Genesis 25:7–10 tells us that when Abraham passed away, both Isaac and Ishmael, his sons, came together to bury him. Despite the treatment Ishmael had endured, he was there to honor his father and ensure he received a proper burial. Ishmael did not dishonor his father by contesting his assets with Isaac, even when there may have been temptation to do so, as there is no direct biblical account of Ishmael formally disputing Isaac's inheritance.

In today's world, many people disrespect their fathers over minor grievances. As you read this, perhaps you're someone who feels your father doesn't deserve your respect, but I believe you haven't experienced what Ishmael went through at the hands of his father.

While some may justify Ishmael's pain as a consequence of God's command, it's important to note that Ishmael may not have even known that God had instructed Abraham to send them away. Despite the Abrahamic covenant being passed through Isaac, God still blessed Ishmael; to this day, his descendants remain. This could be the result of his honoring his father, despite all odds.

Let's look at the power of utterance from the dimension of the drama between Esau and his father, Isaac.

Genesis 27:34-40 [NIV]. "34 When Esau heard these words from his father, he shouted out a very loud and bitter cry and said to his father, "Bless me too, Father!" 35 Isaac said, "Your brother came and deceived me and has taken away your blessing." 36 Esau said, "Isn't that why he's named Jacob? He's cheated me twice already: He took my rights as firstborn, and now he's taken my blessing." So he asked, "Haven't you saved a blessing for me?" 37 Isaac answered Esau, "I have made him your master, and I have made all his brothers serve him. I've provided fresh grain and new wine for him. What is left for me to do for you, Son?" 38 Esau asked, "Do you have only one blessing, Father? Bless me too, Father!" And Esau sobbed loudly. 39 His father Isaac answered him, "The place where you live will lack the fertile fields of the earth and the dew from the sky above. 40 You will use your sword to live, and you will serve your brother. But eventually you will gain your freedom and break his yoke[b] off your neck."

There is a place for a father's blessing, and there is a place for a mother's blessing, we need both to become successful in life. When a father passes away, both of these blessings are then bestowed on the mother. Pronouncements by mothers are equally potent, which is why the Bible emphasizes the need to honor our parents for the promise of longevity. However, if the father is alive, the mother cannot bestow the father's blessing on the children. If this were possible, Rachel would not have gone through the trouble of disguising

Jacob to look like his brother; she would have blessed him herself. Other examples of the spoken word include Christ's encounter with the fig tree, where we can see the consequences of Christ's curse on the fig tree. Even dead Lazarus heard the spoken word.

When Christ read Isaiah 61, He did this in a way that left the people in awe. Luke 4:16-22 [NIV]. "16 He went to Nazareth, where he had been brought up, and on the Sabbath day he went into the synagogue, as was his custom. He stood up to read, 17 and the scroll of the prophet Isaiah was handed to him. Unrolling it, he found the place where it is written: 18 The Spirit of the Lord is on me, because he has anointed me to proclaim good news to the poor. He has sent me to proclaim freedom for the prisoners and recovery of sight for the blind, to set the oppressed free, 19 to proclaim the year of the Lord's favor.[a] 20 Then he rolled up the scroll, gave it back to the attendant and sat down. The eyes of everyone in the synagogue were fastened on him. 21 He began by saying to them, "Today this scripture is fulfilled in your hearing." 22 All spoke well of him and were amazed at the gracious words that came from his lips. "Isn't this Joseph's son?" they asked."

"From the time of the prophet Isaiah to the arrival of Christ, roughly 700 years passed. During that period, many prophets and Pharisees likely read this passage numerous times. However, they always interpreted it as referring to someone else. Christ, on the other hand, read the verse without altering the words, but with a tone that made it clear He was speaking about Himself. You may be facing challenges today, and God's promises for your life might seem impossible due to your current situation. But just as Christ took ownership of what was said about Him, you too can claim the great destiny God has revealed to you. Keep declaring it, and trust that God will bring it to pass.

## Ii. Blood Sacrifice

Blood sacrifice is the most potent of the three, as it has the power to redeem or defy natural laws and change the course of events. God had to shed the blood of His only Son to redeem mankind. He had to kill an animal after the fall of Adam and Eve, and the children of Israel had to kill a lamb to observe the Passover. In all of these instances, blood was shed to make atonement.

I had an uncle who would always argue with my dad that God did not, and cannot, sacrifice His Son for us. He believes in God but just can't bring himself to accept the idea of God sacrificing His Son to redeem us because he feels such an act is too barbaric, and no father would put their child through this.

My uncle had this warm and penetrating gaze that distinguished him from every other person. I remember on one such occasion, he pointed to me while I was sitting next to my dad and asked, 'Are you telling me you can give Bonny up to be sacrificed, or will you put him in the fire because he did not do what you asked of him?'

In truth, my uncle was making a very rational and moral argument, but unfortunately, the way the spirit realm works is beyond reason for the natural man. If I had to provide a response to my late uncle's questions, I would say that if God can give up His Son and look the other way, He can also allow those who, by their own choice, choose hell to go to hell.

Pastor Yomi Olowoyo once said that if only the blood of Christ were required to bring us into salvation, Christ would have shed as much blood as possible but would not have died. The death of Christ is what makes the difference, life for life. His life was taken so that we might have life.

Aside from the fact that God sacrificed His Son, there are other examples where a person was sacrificed just to preserve the life of others. One such example is when the power of blood sacrifice was demonstrated in 2 Kings 3:24–27 [NIV]. When the king of Moab had to sacrifice his firstborn son to turn around a battle he was already losing, in his favor.

"24 But when the Moabites came to the camp of Israel, the Israelites rose up and fought them until they fled. And the Israelites invaded the land and slaughtered the Moabites. 25 They destroyed the towns, and each man threw a stone on every good field until it was covered. They stopped up all the springs and cut down every good tree. Only Kir Hareseth was left with its stones in place, but men armed with slings surrounded it and attacked it. 26 When the king of Moab saw that the battle had gone against him, he took with him seven hundred swordsmen to break through to the king of Edom, but they failed. 27 Then he took his firstborn son, who was to succeed him as king, and offered him as a sacrifice on the city wall. The fury against Israel was great; they withdrew and returned to their own land."

The interesting thing about this battle is that God had already promised the Israelites victory before they set out for battle, and they were winning the battle before the king of Moab made his move. The takeaway from this is that the sacrifice of his son altered something in the spirit realm that changed the direction of the battle. Now, imagine what the sacrifice of Christ, the Son of God, would mean in the spirit realm. Don't we think it can alter the course of events in the physical realm?

Aside from referencing biblical events, there are other modern-day examples where a life was sacrificed to turn events around in the physical realm. One such example happened in Nigeria.

The first Attah (Father) of the independent Igala kingdom is known as Ayegba Om' Idoko (Ayegba the son of Idoko) who led a war of liberation against the Jukun, 1515-1516 culminating in the sacrifice of his daughter, Inikpi to ensure victory. Until date the statue of Inikpi is still standing at her burial spot at Ega market close to river Niger in Idah, Kogi State Nigeria.

If we examine these two examples, the sacrifice made by the king of Moab and the one referenced in Nigeria, we see that both were carried out by kings. These kings had slaves, at the very least, they should have sacrificed their slaves and preserved the heir to the throne. But they did not. Instead, they sacrificed the heir. This pattern has something in common with God giving up His only Son, the Heir, for the redemption of mankind.

If we research further, we will see occurrences of blood sacrifices in Europe and other continents. The difference between Christ's sacrifice and the sacrifices referenced above is that Christ's death is for all of mankind.

It remains a mystery how the sacrifice of a single life, like that of Inikpi or Mesha's heir, the son of the Moabite king, could save tens of thousands from certain death on the battlefield. These individuals were not sinless, yet their deaths carried a power that defies natural understanding. This mystery of **'one for all and all for one'** can only be truly comprehended through a deeper understanding of the events that unfolded in the spiritual realm.

Now imagine Christ, sinless and on His way to the Cross. He set Barabbas, a thief, free. While on the Cross, He offered forgiveness, salvation, and new life to another thief. Then He went into the grave, conquered death, and rose again to offer new life to all of humanity.

All the sacrifices mentioned above, such as those of Inikpi or King Mesha's son, did not culminate in the resurrection of the individuals involved. These were mortal beings, not sinless, and their deaths, while significant, did not transcend death itself. In contrast, what transpired in the realm of death during the three days following Christ's crucifixion, culminating in His defeat of death, sets His sacrifice apart. Christ's story did not end with His death; rather, it was fulfilled through His resurrection and eventual ascension into heaven, marking a unique and transformative event in human history.

Therefore, anyone who believes that Christ's death on the Cross, just one death, holds no personal relevance to them has yet to grasp the profound interplay between the physical world we inhabit and the spiritual realms that govern it.

I remember these lines from a song: 'Jesus paid it all, all to Him I owe; sin had left a crimson stain, He washed it white as snow.' If you reflect deeply on the lines above, these words will surely resonate with you.

The pure blood of the one who knew no sin, sacrificed for a once-and-for-all atonement. The death that resulted in the curtain of the temple being torn in two, implying that no more sacrifices are needed to reconcile us to God. The tearing of the temple curtain is a biblical event that symbolizes the start of a new relationship with God and the end of the old covenant. Access to God is now open to all believers due to Jesus's sacrifice.

Therefore, the blood of Christ was the price paid for every living human being. Christ died for all of mankind, and that grace is available to humanity as a whole. Salvation is right before us, all we have to do is accept it, but God won't force anyone to put their faith in Him. If God compels us to love Him, then it is no longer genuine love.

Just like my late uncle, many critics of the Christian faith, particularly in Western societies, now decry Christ's death on the cross as barbaric. Some have gone as far as saying they cannot serve a God who had to kill His only Son. Unfortunately, those who speak in these terms have no insight into what happens in the realm of the spirit. They have failed to ask themselves if there was an alternative to Christ dying on the cross to redeem mankind.

## Iii. Boundaries

The affairs of the spirit realm are guided by boundaries, whether godly or occult. Balaam's attempt to curse the Israelites was unsuccessful. Each time he opened his mouth to curse, all he could alter was blessings. This is because the Israelites are under the blessings of Abraham. The only help Balaam could offer to Balak was to find a way to lure the Israelites out of the covering of the blessings. They needed to entice the Israelites so they would violate the boundaries set by God. To achieve this, they had to lure the Israelites into the sin of fornication, and inevitably, God had to turn His back on them, as His face cannot behold their sin.

Corinthians 2:14. 14 "The person without the Spirit does not accept the things that come from the Spirit of God but considers them foolishness and cannot understand them because they are discerned only through the Spirit."

Understanding God's heart is crucial for remaining within His boundaries in daily Christian living. Knowing God's character, nature, and will, along with understanding your own identity in Christ, provides clarity and empowers you to set healthy spiritual boundaries, separating the kingdom of God from the kingdom of the world.

It is not up to God to seek the heart of man, rather, it is up to man to seek the heart of God. In seeking the heart of God, He will direct our path and give us insight into His thoughts, and this will, in turn, help to further our relationship with Him. However, Bro. Gbile Akanni emphasized that we cannot discount the literary interpretation of the Word of God, even as we seek to understand its spiritual interpretation. The literary interpretation is the starting point, but this must not be taken out of context.

There are several places in the bible where the Pharisees took Jesus's words literally and in these cases, they were taken out of context. John 2:19 where Jesus said He will rebuild the church in 3 days. John 3:3 where Jesus said unless one is born again he cannot see the kingdom of God. John 8:58 "Jesus told them, "I can guarantee this truth: Before Abraham was ever born, I am."

Ephesians 6:12 reminds us that we do not wrestle against flesh and blood. When it comes to boundaries, the Bible acknowledges that God places a protective hedge around a person's life, as seen in His conversation with Satan about Job. I've often seen this quote displayed in many Christian homes, and it resonates deeply: "Christ is the head of the home, the unseen guest at every meal, the silent listener to every conversation." This speaks to the spiritual protection that God has placed around a home. The enemy's only goal is clear: if someone is not in Christ, keep them away from Him; if they are in Christ, pull them away from Him. This is where a solid understanding of the spiritual realm and how it helps a person stay within God's covering becomes crucial.

In a recent sit down with Pastor Yomi Olowoyo, he said there are no accidents in the spirit realm as he pointed out that it wasn't just coincidence that Simeon was in the temple when Mary and Joseph brought Jesus to the temple to be consecrated to the Lord.

Therefore. even as we study the Bible as our guide, we still need daily direction from God in our walk with Him today. This will go a long way in keeping us within God's boundaries, and it is only possible if our spiritual antenna is switched on.

# CHAPTER FIFTEEN

## *He makes diviners mad*

The Bible describes how God makes diviners mad by exposing their false prophecies and making them look foolish. Isaiah 44:25 (New Century Version) says, "I show that the signs of the lying prophets are false; I make fools of those who do magic. I confuse even the wise; they think they know much, but I make them look foolish."

Have you paused to meditate on the mystery of how God works? He gave birth to His Son, Jesus, in a manger, against the popular expectation for the birth of a king. Moreover, Jesus died in a manner that even His disciples did not expect, even though He had been speaking about His death all along in parables. In the same way, Christ's return will happen against the popular expectations of a world that sees Christianity as a myth.

Everything about Christ was, and still is, a mystery. His coming to earth to live among mankind caught many scholars unaware, despite hundreds of years of prophecies about His coming. While the people expected a royal birth, He arrived in a manger. They expected Him to associate with the rulers of the day; instead, He associated with the sick, poor, and needy. They expected Him to show the fullness of His power; instead, He showed them His vulnerable side. They expected Him to make Himself clearer; instead,

He spoke to them in parables. He was a king without ordination and had no physical palace. Christ was innocent, but the people preferred to set a thief free and wanted the innocent to die in place of the thief. Jesus was born in a borrowed manger and buried in a borrowed tomb.

It wasn't about shouting the scrawled five-letter word 'Jesus' that makes a person a Christian, but believing wholeheartedly in what the name can do and the power behind the name.

The Pharisees, who understood the Torah back-to-back and were looking forward to the fulfillment of the prophecy, had no knowledge that the prophecy had already been fulfilled. The King they were waiting for was the man standing right in front of them. They were able to confirm the prophecy to King Herod, yet remained oblivious to the mystery surrounding its fulfillment.

Matt 2: 3 When King Herod heard this he was disturbed, and all Jerusalem with him. 4 When he had called together all the people's chief priests and teachers of the law, he asked them where the Messiah was to be born. 5 "In Bethlehem in Judea," they replied, "for this is what the prophet has written:

6 "'But you, Bethlehem, in the land of Judah, are by no means least among the rulers of Judah; for out of you will come a ruler who will shepherd my people Israel".

The Pharisees were following Christ literally and in the flesh, but they were not following in the spirit. That was why they lacked the spiritual discernment to recognize that His coming had been fulfilled. It is therefore important to have a personal relationship with Christ, a relationship that operates in the spirit realm. Unfortunately, just as the Pharisees were caught off guard, many who serve God in the flesh will suffer the same fate as the Pharisees. The following Bible verses give us an indication of what Christ's return will look like and what it will mean for those not worshiping in truth and in spirit: Revelation 16:15, Matthew 24:43, 1 Thessalonians 5:2, 1 Thessalonians 5:4, and 2 Peter 3:10.

Revelation 16:15 says, 'Behold, I am coming like a thief! Blessed is the one who stays awake, keeping his garments on, that he may not go about naked and be seen exposed!

Someone like Simeon who aligned with the happenings in the spirit realm, knew of the arrival of the Messiah, but the Pharisees and Sadducees, who were acclaimed to be the custodians of the Torah, had no knowledge that the Torah had been fulfilled. Do we think we have known all that is needed to know about God, or are we still seeking? I think I would prefer the latter. This is because Christ said those who seek will find, not just seeking, but seeking with a humble heart.

Luke 2: 25-32. 25 "At that time there was a man in Jerusalem named Simeon. He was righteous and devout and was eagerly waiting for the Messiah to come and rescue Israel. The Holy Spirit was upon him 26 and had revealed to him that he would not die until he had seen the Lord's Messiah. 27 That day the Spirit led him to the Temple. So when Mary and Joseph came to present the baby Jesus to the Lord as the law required, 28 Simeon was there. He took the child in his arms and praised God, saying, 29 "Sovereign Lord, now let your servant die in peace, as you have promised.

30 I have seen your salvation, 31 which you have prepared for all people.

32 He is a light to reveal God to the nations, and he is the glory of your people Israel!"

How much do you think you know about God? Would you rely on your intelligence, based on what you know about the world around you, in your dealings with God, or would you be like David, who at the slightest opportunity would request the Ephod so he could inquire of the Lord?

## Light in the Last Days

Moreover, the three wise men from the East were aware of the birth of the Messiah, whereas the Jews, unto whom Christ was born, had no knowledge that the Messiah was already in their midst. These wise men knew they were coming to worship a baby, and interestingly, they described the baby as a king, which explains their level of insight.

Even though Christ had not announced His mission at the time of His birth, these men had insight into His birth, life, and death, as explained by their gifts. It is reasonable to conclude that the three wise men from the East, who were Gentiles, were the first believers in Christ, a mystery difficult to explain.

The Bible says God warned the three wise men in a dream not to return to King Herod because Herod intended to harm the baby Jesus. They knew it was God speaking, they obeyed, and did not return to King Herod. The Jews would find it hard to imagine that their God would speak to the Chaldeans. The truth is, the Pharisees are blinded by their head knowledge of the Torah and have lost touch with what is happening in the spirit realm. God will always use someone who understands when He is speaking and will obey to the letter.

# CHAPTER SIXTEEN

*Remaining attached in difficult times*

People all over the world can't understand why Christians follow Jesus. The truth is that a relationship with Christ is one laced in mystery, which the ordinary human mind can't fathom. Those who have succeeded in establishing a personal relationship with Christ can feel His existence, His presence, and their connection with God, but the foundation of this relationship is based on our love for God. Obviously, a relationship with God is mutual and not obligatory. This dynamic goes beyond mere spiritual fantasy, and the tangibility of the relationship is very real for those who put the will of God ahead of their own.

Interestingly, a relationship with Christ is one forged in the fires of obedience, faith, and personal connection.

Natalie Bassy, a popular Nigerian gospel singer, once said, "Faith is not normal," because you will find yourself acting contrary to conventional wisdom, which might make people consider your actions as lacking in common sense.

People continue to wonder why Christians who go through one challenge or another continue to trust in Jesus Christ, even in the midst of their storm. Moreover, even when the storm is over and their prayer isn't answered, and the worst happens, they still put their faith in God. The world is rattled by the Christian faith. A Christian loses an eye, and he thanks God for the one eye left. A Christian loses a child, and he or she thanks God for the children left, and even when they lose all their assets to fire, they still thank God for escaping the fire alive.

This level of unalloyed devotion to God dumbfounds non-Christians, and as a result, most atheists have come to conclude that devoted Christians have passed the point of reasoned discussion.

I listened to Mel Gibson's interview shortly after the complete loss of his home to the destructive Los Angeles wildfire of January 2025. Typical of Christians, Mel's response was that he feels what happened to him was a kind of purification by God, and he believes God was stripping him of what he had to prepare him for something big. This "something big" isn't about making big money, but about taking on a God-given project. Though he described his ordeal as a mixture of sadness, realization, and, of course, a blessing, he said, 'God gives, God takes; we are here with nothing, and that is the same way we go out. But here's the deal: you will always be okay if you seek first the kingdom of God.'

The fact that devoted Christians continue trusting in God in the midst of their storm does not mean they do not feel pain, hollowed out, or heartbroken, they do. They grieve, and they sometimes feel disappointed in God, yet they find strength to remain in faith. This is because they have come to understand that if God allows something to happen, there is nothing they can do about it.

However, the feeling of being let down by God when something bad happens is not exclusive to unbelivers. Non-Christians, lukewarm Christians, and even devoted Christians sometimes share this feeling.

I must confess, I know that feeling. I felt so depressed and emotional when I lost my immediate elder brother in 2017. I couldn't understand why God allowed my brother to die, despite our prayers for God's intervention.

I remember vividly that within the first few days after my brother's death, each time my wife raised the prayer point, 'Let's thank God for keeping us alive and for what He's doing in our lives' during our daily devotion, subconsciously, I would freeze and become speechless. The thought that immediately came to mind was, 'Thank God for allowing my brother to die?' I usually remained in this frozen state until my wife moved to the next prayer point. Just like Mel Gibson, I had to come face to face with the sadness of losing my brother before realizing that my brother is dead and there is nothing I can do about it. In the days that followed, I found myself praying again to God, thanking Him for life and even committing my late brother's children to God.

Some Christians, driven by extreme vanity, equate being a good Christian with having abundance, claiming that God isn't responsible for your pain or lack. They assert that when you're in need, it has nothing to do with God. While it's true that the Bible says God desires for us to prosper and be in good health, it also teaches that trials exist to test our faith, to determine whether it is strong and pure, just as fire refines and purifies gold. These aren't just words; they are the very tools that help a person grow in faith.

The story of the woman with a small jar of oil is one of a person going through trials. Much focus has been placed on the woman's failure to acknowledge that she had something when Elijah asked her what she had in her house. In one of his sermons, Ken Gott shed more light on this story. He examined it from the perspective of a person serving the Lord diligently and how this can sometimes result in our disappointment with God.

2 Kings 4:1 "The wife of a man from the company of the prophets cried out to Elisha, "Your servant my husband is dead,

*Light in the Last Days*

and you know that he revered the LORD. But now his creditor is coming to take my two boys as his slaves."

Considering the passage from 2 Kings 6:1-7, where the sons of the prophets asked Elisha to accompany them as they sought to expand their living space, it can be inferred that these sons of the prophets were likely part of a ministry school, living together in a communal setting. In today's terms, we could liken them to students preparing for pastoral ministry. Furthermore, it's possible that the loan in question was taken out as part of his desire to attend a pastoral training school.

There is no question about this man's diligence, and Elisha did not refute her claim. However, the focus of her claim was on the words 'Your servant.' She is presenting to God that His servant, not just anyone's servant, but God's servant, died prematurely, and his family is now in crisis. While the late prophet may have made a poor choice in using his sons as collateral for a loan, that was not her concern. She was not accusing her husband of a lapse in judgment. Her cry was that of a woman telling God, 'We have served You diligently and do not deserve this.' This reinforces the fact that bad things sometimes happen to good people. Good Christians can sometimes die unexpectedly young. The question here is the big picture, which lies with God. As humans, we tend to focus on our immediate circumstances, while God might have other reasons for allowing the prophet's death. God has used this story of the late prophet's family to show us His ability to turn a difficult situation around and demonstrate that heaven's resources are not limited, as the oil did not stop flowing until they ran out of jars.

John the Baptist equally felt let down by Christ during his incarceration in the hands of King Herod, he expected that Jesus Christ being the Son of God should have come to his rescue.

That was what made him send his disciples to Jesus to ask if He is the one to come. (Mathew 11: 2-6) "2 When John, who was in prison, heard about the deeds of the Messiah, he sent his disciples 3 to ask him, "Are you the one who is to come, or should we expect someone else? 4 Jesus replied, "Go back and report to John what you hear and see: 5 The blind receive sight, the lame walk, those who have leprosy[a] are cleansed, the deaf hear, the dead are raised, and the good news is proclaimed to the poor. 6 Blessed is anyone who does not stumble on account of me."

Despite the fact that John the Baptist talked about the coming of Jesus Christ, when he said to the Pharisees, the one who comes after Him is the Messiah and the straps of whose sandals he is not worthy to untie. He is equally the same prophet who announced Jesus to the world, (John 1:29, The next day he saw Jesus coming toward him, and said, "Behold, the Lamb of God, who takes away the sin of the world).

The ensuing argument between John the Baptist and Jesus Christ about who should baptize whom emphasizes the extent of John's knowledge of Jesus Christ's identity as the Messiah (Matthew 3:14-15). But John tried to deter Him, saying, "I need to be baptized by You, and do You come to me?" Jesus replied, "Let it be so now; it is proper for us to do this to fulfill all righteousness." Then John consented.

Jesus Christ also felt the same during His darkest hour. He cried, "My God, my God, why have You forsaken Me?" even though He knew and had spoken about this moment in advance before it actually happened. There is nothing wrong with being emotional when something bad happens to us. The feeling of being let down by God is not exclusive to you, that is what makes us human. Even Jesus Christ and John the Baptist felt the same in their darkest hours, but what matters most is that they did not turn away from their faith and did not walk away from their cross.

It is possible that our hurt comes from how badly people have treated us, and we may ask God, "Why did You allow this to happen?" The two disciples Christ encountered on the road to Emmaus felt quite hopeless as they saw Christ die in such a hopeless manner, and this affected them to the point of forgetting what the Bible said about Christ's resurrection (Luke 24:13-35).

They saw that the people prefer the thief, Barabbas, to be freed and Christ, the innocent one, to be crucified. Just like many in our world today, they saw the injustice being done, but they did not see hope for the victim and did not recognize Christ as the one who would judge the world and make every victim whole again. But when their eyes were opened, their hope was restored. I will therefore urge you to pray for insight concerning that matter which seems hopeless.

On the other hand, our hurt might be a result of the things we have done, and our lives may have been hollowed out due to guilt, leaving us unable to move on with life. For those of us hurting, it is important to note that God is justice, the righteous Judge, and He is also merciful. The interesting thing is that God possesses both justice and mercy in ample measure.

It is important to emphasize that we should be careful not to let our circumstances keep us angry or detached from God for too long. This is because when we do, we may slip away, become more vulnerable, and play into the hands of the devil. Consequently, if we don't find a way to retrace our steps back to God, we could find ourselves taking actions that bring us more trouble and that is exactly where the devil wants us to be.

Cain was angry and disappointed in God for rejecting his offering, and he brooded over the matter for so long that it eventually led to him killing his brother out of envy. The time between the offering and when God cautioned Cain about his anger and the eventual murder of his brother was probably long enough for Cain to shake off his hurt. Killing his brother was exactly where the devil wanted him to be and the devil succeeded.

This brings to mind Dr. R.T. Kendall's message titled "Forgive God," where the man of God encouraged us to understand God in those moments when our expectations are not met. His context of "forgiving God" wasn't because God had done something wrong, but because there is often more to our unmet expectations than we can understand, and we might not grasp God's reasons at the time.

There is no need to throw the baby out with the bathwater. God is the real deal, and we must avoid any action that would sever our relationship with Him.

It doesn't matter how we feel about God, He has the final say, and His decision is absolute. Through prayer, we can stop the devil's attacks on our lives, and who better to turn to for help than God?

The devil is a formidable adversary and should not be taken lightly. The only true source of hope and deliverance for anyone facing his schemes is God. The devil does not relent, and he will not stop unless God intervenes on our behalf. Therefore, I urge us never to let anger or frustration keep us from running to God for help, because the enemy will not cease his attacks.

There is a story my father once told me about a great hunter from my hometown. A prophecy was given that he would be killed by a bull. To avoid this fate, he decided to stop hunting bulls altogether. Instead, he would relax in an easy chair in front of his house, where a large bull skull hung overhead. One day, as fate would have it, the string holding the skull snapped, and it fell, striking him on the forehead, killing him instantly.

The devil did not stop after tempting Christ once, he persisted a second time, a third, and continued even after Christ overcame him. He pressed on relentlessly, all the way to the crucifixion. This is something the hunter may not have fully understood.

As I mentioned earlier, the devil never gives up, and our human wisdom, just like that of this hunter, is not enough to restrain him. The only power that can restrain the devil is God. Let's not allow our frustration with God to push us away from the only One who can truly help us.

You may have been wronged and may have genuine reasons to be angry, but it is important not to allow victimhood to overwhelm us. Just like Cain, who allowed himself to be overtaken by anger because God favored his brother over him. Instead of turning a new leaf and doing things better, he played the victim, and that resulted in his brother's death. We may not kill someone in our own case, but we might end up taking actions that don't please God.

It's important that we make a conscious effort to deal with hurt, bitterness, and things like unforgiveness, as these little foxes, as the Bible describes them, can easily sever our relationship with God without us even knowing it.

The Bible refers to certain sins as little foxes. Even though sin is sin by God's standard, this is because there is a tendency not to regard some of our actions as sin, even when they offend God. Things like unforgiveness, bearing false witness, and backbiting can linger in a person's soul and remain unnoticed. Our soul carries emotion, and in most cases, we think we are in control of what goes on within us, but in reality, we aren't.

Understanding how our subconscious works matters a lot. For example, there are times when you see someone while you are going about your day, maybe at the bus stop, supermarket, or even in a movie and try to place the face. As you try to recollect where you saw that person or how you know them, and after trying for a while without success, you forget about it. However, hours later, or after you have retired for the day, you suddenly remember and are now able to place the face, recalling the movie or where you saw the person last. Interestingly, you might have forgotten about trying to place the face in that moment, but your mind didn't. It would continue to subconsciously search in an attempt to place that face. Every one of us experiences this, and the above example shows that our souls do not forget, even after we have left a matter. Therefore, we must put our subconscious in check because our soul won't let go of certain issues in life, particularly when they relate to hurt, if we do not make a conscious effort to deal with them.

The devil does not think he has had the best of you, despite your current troubles. If left alone, he desires to cause you more and more trouble. That is why we cannot allow ourselves to slip away from God's hand, even at a time when we feel God has let us down. Considering the life of Job, the devil did not stop at destroying his business. He proceeded to take Job's children from him, and as if destroying his business and killing his children was not enough, the devil took Job's health away. If not for God and the hedge around Job's life, the devil would have proceeded to take Job's life. Similarly, the devil did not only separate the prodigal son from his father, but he brought him so low that he ended up eating food meant for swine. The devil would have tormented him further until he took his life, but grace located him when he came to his senses and returned to his father.

Our hurt might also be the result of hardship, things are just not panning out, despite our hard work. I encourage you to continue holding on until God comes through for you. Just remember that there is no mountain God can't climb and no door God can't kick down to come to your rescue. Maybe the time for your manifestation is just a little while longer. David also felt frustrated when he was hiding in caves and running from King Saul, who sought to kill him. God had to reassure David by telling him He would put the king at David's mercy, just to prove to David that He hadn't forgotten him and God did.

It is God's desire that we prosper, but our prosperity is sometimes located at certain crossroads in our lives. These crossroads might require sacrifice in the form of discipline and holding onto our faith in God to make it to the other side where our prosperity lies.

*Light in the Last Days*

Genesis 1:28 (NIV): God blessed them and said to them, "Be fruitful and increase in number; fill the earth and subdue it. Rule over the fish in the sea and the birds in the sky and over every living creature that moves on the ground."

Considering the above verse, we can conclude that it is God's desire for humans to be fruitful, but they must subdue and dominate the earth. Some versions of the Bible interchange the word "subdue" with "dominate." Irrespective of which word is used, both "dominate" and "subdue" are verbs, and they are action words. Ordinarily, one cannot subdue another without putting in some effort to bring the other under control.

Therefore, in all facets of life, whether in space travel, engineering, medicine, administration, or even in our relationships, we are all expected to put in effort to bring out the beauty that God intended."

In Joshua 5:12, the manna ceased on the very day that Israel was able to eat from the produce of the land of Canaan. Even though the milk and honey God referred to were metaphorical, relating to the fertility of the land rather than actual milk and honey, the Israelites had to cultivate the land to make the promise of milk and honey a reality in their lives.

Consequently, overcoming challenges is a part of life, as this brings about the beauty God had in mind for mankind. The quotation below by Jordan Peterson provides some illumination on how humans are wired:

"We are built to walk uphill, and when we reach the pinnacle of the hill, we want to stop and appreciate the view. But the next thing we want is a higher hill at a distance, and it is the uphill climb that we derive our value from."

This desire to conquer another hill is an emotion filled with enthusiasm, and Jordan Peterson relates this enthusiasm to come from God. He proceeds to say that our lives become richer and more abundant as we overcome challenges in the pursuit of our goals. He describes the virtue and goal derived from the pursuit as transcendent, placing this above everything we do.

There is a difference between overcoming challenges to achieve a set goal and going through difficult times. Overcoming challenges and living in hardship or difficulties might not be the same, but sometimes the outcome might be the same: to bring us closer to our purpose. God might sometimes deny us progress on our desired path or allow difficulties in our lives just to make us change course.

Isaiah 43:19 [NIV]. "See, I am doing a new thing! Now it springs up; do you not perceive it? I am making a way in the wilderness and streams in the wasteland."

That moment the slave trader's fetters reached the feet of Joseph might be interpreted to mean the end, but as far as God is concerned, He was doing a new thing in Joseph's life.

All the dreams Joseph had about a great future, where his dad and brothers would bow to him, had been dormant until he ended up in the hands of slave traders bound for Egypt. His destiny was set in Egypt, but he had been living in Canaan with his dad at the time, until his brothers' betrayal set him on course for Egypt, where his future lay.

In like manner, the moment Potiphar's wife lied about Joseph, resulting in his being sent to prison where he came into contact with the butler, that was God doing a new thing in Joseph's life.

This reminds me of a message by Archbishop Benson Idahosa titled "Knock Down for A Lifting Up." His message sheds more light on how God works most of the time. Except in a few cases where our success comes like a burst of sunshine, God often knocks down what we stand on or takes away what we have, just to set us on the path He has in mind for us. Understandably, this process is never palatable because it often comes with heartaches.

Therefore, when God said, "I am doing a new thing! Now it springs up; do you not perceive it?" it means that what God is doing is ongoing and has not yet reached completion. Sometimes, it is only when God completes what He is doing in our lives that we will have a clearer picture of what God is about. The question, "Do you not perceive it?" that God asked, is an indication that there is a possibility we might not perceive the knocking-down process as God doing a new thing in our lives. Joseph only understood why he was sold to the slave traders by the time he ended up as Prime Minister.

The "knocking down," in the eyes of an ordinary person, might be interpreted as failure or being abandoned by God, despite our total devotion to Him. However, this might be God saying, "I am doing a new thing" in your life. It is therefore essential for us as Christians to go on our knees to seek God's face and inquire of His view on our current circumstance. With this, we can know when to hold on fast and trust in Him as we go through turbulent times, or when to pray for God to turn our circumstance around, because not all negative situations are about God doing a new thing.

There are times in our lives when it becomes clear that we are holding on by a thread, and yet, God comes through for us. It is therefore important that we count our blessings one by one, because in doing so, we begin to truly appreciate the many miracles God has already done in our lives. Counting our blessings is not about ignoring our challenges, but about refusing to let the bad times overshadow the memories of the good. This doesn't minimize the importance of our unanswered prayers, rather, it strengthens our hope in God.

Christ's comment in the book of John 5:14 indicates that the man's illness was the result of his sin. It is important to note, however, that while some difficulties in life may be the consequence of our bad choices, this is not always the case.

Job 8:1-6 NLT gave us a little insight into how a person going through difficulties may erroneously be perceived to be the cause of their problem.

"1 Then Bildad the Shuhite replied to Job: 2 "How long will you go on like this? You sound like a blustering wind. 3 Does God twist justice? Does the Almighty twist what is right? 4 Your children must have sinned against him, so their punishment was well deserved. 5 But if you pray to God and seek the Favor of the Almighty, 6 and if you are pure and live with integrity, he will surely rise up and restore your happy home."

There are many Christians today who think the same way as Bildad the Shuhite: "If things are hard for you, then maybe it is your fault." If you are trying for a child and remain unsuccessful, then maybe you haven't fasted and prayed enough. If you are sick and do not recover, perhaps you haven't prayed hard enough. If a Christian dies prematurely, maybe they weren't faithful enough in their walk with God. If you suffer financial loss or lose your job, then maybe you are not fulfilling your covenant practices, such as giving offerings or paying tithes.

As Christians, it's understandable to seek meaning in difficult situations. However, if we are too quick to assume that it is always God's will for us to remain sick, barren, or die prematurely, we risk undermining the very faith we are called to have in God's healing, provision, and sovereignty.

Importantly, the mindset that someone must have done something wrong or isn't a "good enough" Christian if they're experiencing hardship can be deeply damaging. This is because it can cause people to isolate themselves or hide their struggles out of fear of judgment, and that does not help the body of Christ. As the old proverb says, "Those who hear not the music think the dancer is mad." It is therefore crucial that we seek to understand rather than judge.

Just as God was with Joseph and David in the midst of their trials, He can also be with Christians today as they face difficulties. It's easy to think that the stories of Job, Joseph, and David only apply to biblical times, but that's not the case. Even now, there are many faithful Christians who are suffering, even being martyred in hostile nations, yet God is with them, even until the end.

Being a Christian does not mean a life without trouble. In the same way, living righteously does not guarantee a trouble-free life. Jehoshaphat served the Lord faithfully, yet armies still waged war against him. Therefore, what trusting God does is help us navigate our difficulties, not necessarily remove them.

The acceptance or rejection of God does not take pain out of our path. Life itself is a mystery, without a formula. We are all on unique journeys, and sometimes, even when our choices are the same, our outcomes differ. The difference often lies in the level of grace available to each individual. And at times, our level of grace is not necessarily dependent on how close we are to God. We've seen faithful Christians die young, this too is part of the mystery of God. This mystery is what keeps both "him that standeth" and even the unbelieving from putting their faith in themselves, but instead encourages all to work out their salvation daily. With God, every day is a school day. A walk with God requires daily guidance from the Holy Spirit.

Often, we want God to take us out of our troubles. But in many cases, God leaves us in the midst of them. Even so, He walks us through those troubles and glorifies His name through our circumstances.

Moreover, not all our struggles come from external attacks, sometimes they result from careless lifestyle choices that leave us feeling ashamed or guilty. Don't let guilt and shame push you away from God. Don't think God wouldn't want anything to do with you because of how ugly your sin may seem. The only thing guilt and shame truly accomplish is driving us further from God until, eventually, we feel cut off, and the grace to return feels lost. Even then, it's vital to make a conscious effort to turn away from the lifestyle that brought on the guilt and shame in the first place.

Many people, Christians and nonbelievers alike are burdened with the question. Why would a good God allow pain and so much evil in the world? The answer to our pain lies with God. He alone knows why person "A" suffers while person "B" is spared, even when their circumstances appear the same.

However, pain either pushes us away from God or draws us closer to Him, but in most cases, it is the very thing that draws us back to God. The pain from our careless choices has the potential to produce a lifestyle of restraint. The difficulties experienced by the prodigal son, down to the point of sharing food with swine, were what propelled him to crawl back to his father. That is what pain does: it brings us back to God.

As for the evil in the world, the Bible has already stated that this world will pass away along with its desires. It is merely a short transit point for us as humans.

Romans 8:35 NKJV "Who shall separate us from the love of Christ? shall tribulation, or distress, or persecution, or famine, or nakedness, or peril, or sword?"

The truth remains that God created man to worship Him and does not share His glory with anyone. Therefore, if we are for God, it's either "God's way or God's way," there is no room for man's way, unless we choose to go our own way entirely.

God remains God, He cannot be dethroned, replaced, or subjected to human scrutiny. Our emotions and anger toward God do not change the fact that we are human and He is God. What we think of Him does not diminish who He is in any way. Job 13:15 NKJ. "Though he slay me, yet will I trust in him: but I will maintain mine own ways before him." Just like Job, let's continue to hold on to God even in those moments when we feel let down.

# CHAPTER SEVENTEEN

*The God that would always say, yes*

Becoming an attested child of God is not easily achieved, but rest assured, you will encounter Satan at the crossroads where your faith will be tested.

Yes, the devil might be at the crossroads, yes, we might be tested, but we certainly have a God who says, 'Call on Me, and I will answer you.'

The Bible says, "Ask and it will be given to you; seek and you will find; knock and the door will be opened to you" (Matthew 7:7, NIV). "You do not receive because you do not ask" (James 4:2–3).

When the three sisters went to Moses to request their share of the inheritance, God granted their request. At one point, the Israelites preferred that God speak to them directly and their request was granted. And when they changed their minds about hearing directly from God, He honored that request as well.

When Samson's mother asked the angel to return at a time when her husband would be present, her request was granted. Gideon made several requests to the angel, and God remained patient with him throughout.

Lot said he preferred the valley of Sodom, even though God knew the mountain would be better for him, yet God still granted his request.

Elisha requested a double portion of Elijah's power, and he received exactly what he asked for.

The problem with humans, even the most devoted among us, is that we often have a limited imagination of how far God can go. Although we acknowledge that God's power is unlimited, we ourselves frequently place a ceiling on it. But God's approach is simple: "Make your request, and I will match it."

In 2 Kings 4:1–7, the oil continued to pour for as long as there were jars to collect it.

According to the Bible, in 2 Kings 13:18, Elisha told the king of Israel to "strike the ground" as a symbolic act to signify the extent of the victory he would have over the enemy. The king struck the ground three times with arrows in hand. However, Elisha was upset because he believed the king should have struck the ground more times to represent a more complete victory.

The king may have thought to himself that three victories were the most God could grant them, but the prophet's reaction revealed God's ability to give as many victories as they were willing to believe for.

Despite his failures, Samson made one last request to God, to die with the Philistines and God granted his request. If he had asked for something else, like freedom or the restoration of his sight, perhaps God would have granted that instead. God could have spared Samson's life if he had asked, and it wouldn't have been difficult for God to use something, even a pillar to save him from his fate.

After all, in the days of Rahab the prostitute, when the wall of Jericho fell, the portion of the wall where Rahab's home was located remained standing.

## Light in the Last Days

When Peter saw Christ walking on water and asked if he should come, Christ honoured the request. Matthew 14:28-30 [NIV]. "Lord, if it's you," Peter replied, "tell me to come to you on the water. 29 "Come," he said. Then Peter got down out of the boat, walked on the water and came toward Jesus. 30 But when he saw the wind, he was afraid and, beginning to sink, cried out, "Lord, save me!"

It is God's desire that we be happy. The first thing God did after creating man was to bless humanity, and the last thing He did through Christ, before ascending to heaven was also to bless mankind. This explains the heart of God towards humans. 3 John 1-2 KJV "Beloved, I wish above all things that thou mayest prosper and be in health, even as thy soul prospereth."

Many times, we worry about the future and forget to enjoy the present moment. Interestingly, when that future finally arrives, we often realize there are new concerns that suddenly occupy our minds. God's desire for us to prosper and live in peace was re-emphasized by Christ in Matthew 6:34 [NIV]. "Therefore, do not worry about tomorrow, for tomorrow will worry about itself. Each day has enough trouble of its own."

God is our Creator and our Father, who understands our human nature, how we often focus our concerns on the future and fail to enjoy the present. The Bible makes it clear that God specifically instructed the Israelites not to store manna overnight. This was to teach them to rely on Him daily and not to worry about tomorrow. In this passage, Christ was emphasizing the same principle. In truth, as long as the Israelites continued to depend on God, the manna never ceased during their time in the wilderness. He makes so much goodness available to us daily, yet we tend not to see it because we are overwhelmed by worries, not only about the present but also about what lies ahead.

Let's consider a hypothetical situation:

A young man has just graduated from college or university. He becomes preoccupied with securing a good job and finding the right spouse. Years later, when he finally achieves these milestones, he realizes that his constant worrying had prevented him from enjoying his bachelorhood and the freedom that came with it.

Now married, he recalls the biblical verse, "He who finds a wife finds a good thing," but instead of cherishing this blessing, he becomes consumed with the desire to have children. The joy of being a young couple in love is overshadowed by anxiety. Intimacy becomes merely a means to achieve pregnancy, and when conception doesn't happen as expected, frustration begins to set in.

Eventually, children come along, and new worries take over concerns about their future, education, and well-being. In striving to secure the best for them, he unintentionally misses out on their childhood moments and the opportunity to create lasting memories.

As the years pass, the children grow up and complete their studies. Now, his focus shifts to their choice of spouse. Before he knows it, he has become a grandparent. Looking back, he regrets not fully appreciating each stage of life, enjoying his wife, spending more quality time with his children, and worrying less about the future.

Our careers, our spouses, and the well-being of our families are all significant aspects of life that require attention and God is fully aware of this. He wants us to pursue these things, but not at the cost of missing out on the daily blessings before us. Instead of being weighed down by worry, we should embrace and enjoy the goodness found in each moment.

We have to enjoy the moment by truly living in the moment. A quote from UCB -Word for Today says, "I wished to live deliberately... and not, when I came to die, discover I had not lived."

Our sojourn on earth is short. A hundred years may seem like a lifetime, but in the eyes of God, it is still brief. What matters most is God's desire for us to enjoy His peace in every moment of our lives here on earth. Enjoying a peaceful life is not the result of having plenty, but rather the outcome of a life anchored in God.

We live in a world where people are becoming increasingly disillusioned. Faced with disappointments and uncontrolled inflation, many who placed their faith in their governments are now losing hope in life. According to UK statistics from 2022, suicide is the leading cause of death for men under the age of 50, not sickness, disease, or accidents, but suicide. This is a disheartening reality.

Suicide is often the result of people feeling fed up with life. Imagine teenagers, fifteen or sixteen-year olds who have access to nearly every gadget that should bring them joy, yet they feel hopeless. These kids, in most cases, are not hungry, and they are not sick. They have access to some of the best amenities, a life that many children their age in developing countries only dream of and still, they are weary of life.

This clearly shows that living in abundance does not always lead to fulfillment. True fulfillment comes from remaining hopeful in difficult moments and trusting that they will eventually pass.

Sometimes, I take out time to meditate on the content of Charlie Chaplin's famous speech in the movie, "the great dictator," in 1940. This is one of the most sensible speeches in the history of mankind. It reads thus...

"I'm sorry, but I don't want to be an emperor. That's not my business. I don't want to rule or conquer anyone. I should like to help everyone—if possible—Jew, Gentile—black man—white. We all want to help one another. Human beings are like that. We want to live by each other's happiness—not by each other's misery. We don't want to hate and despise one another. In this world there is room for everyone. And the good earth is rich and can provide for everyone. The way of life can be free and beautiful, but we have lost the way.

## Boniface Ossai

Greed has poisoned men's souls, has barricaded the world with hate, has goose-stepped us into misery and bloodshed. We have developed speed, but we have shut ourselves in. Machinery that gives abundance has left us in want. Our knowledge has made us cynical. Our cleverness, hard and unkind. We think too much and feel too little. More than machinery we need humanity. More than cleverness we need kindness and gentleness. Without these qualities, life will be violent, and all will be lost...

The aeroplane and the radio have brought us closer together. The very nature of these inventions cries out for the goodness in men—cries out for universal brotherhood—for the unity of us all. Even now my voice is reaching millions throughout the world—millions of despairing men, women, and little children—victims of a system that makes men torture and imprison innocent people.

To those who can hear me, I say—do not despair. The misery that is now upon us is but the passing of greed—the bitterness of men who fear the way of human progress. The hate of men will pass, and dictators die, and the power they took from the people will return to the people. And so long as men die, liberty will never perish...

Soldiers! don't give yourselves to brutes—men who despise you—enslave you—who regiment your lives—tell you what to do—what to think and what to feel! Who drill you—diet you—treat you like cattle, use you as cannon fodder. Don't give yourselves to these unnatural men—machine men with machine minds and machine hearts! You are not machines! You are not cattle! You are men! You have the love of humanity in your hearts! You don't hate! Only the unloved hate—the unloved and the unnatural! Soldiers! Don't fight for slavery! Fight for liberty!

In the 17th Chapter of St Luke it is written: "the Kingdom of God is within man"—not one man nor a group of men, but in all men! In you! You, the people, have the power—the power to create machines. The power to create happiness! You, the people, have the power to make this life free and beautiful, to make this life a wonderful adventure.

Then—in the name of democracy—let us use that power—let us all unite. Let us fight for a new world—a decent world that will give men a chance to work—that will give youth a future and old age a security. By the promise of these things, brutes have risen to power. But they lie! They do not fulfill that promise. They never will!

Dictators free themselves but they enslave the people! Now let us fight to fulfil that promise! Let us fight to free the world—to do away with national barriers—to do away with greed, with hate and intolerance. Let us fight for a world of reason, a world where science and progress will lead to all men's happiness. Soldiers! in the name of democracy, let us all unite!"

Unfortunately, 85 years later, despite humanity having made several advancements in economics, technology, medicine, food production, artificial intelligence, and more, our lives remain miserable and sad. The world we live in today is eerily familiar, if not worse than the one described by Charlie Chaplin. Despite the reduction in the rate of global poverty, we still witness wars, crises of all kinds, and a skyrocketing suicide rate. This serves as a testament to the fact that, without God, we cannot lead a fulfilled life.

Come to think of the story of the Samaritan woman at the well who had been married five times. Marrying as many as five husbands in such a culture at the time was rare. Comparing this woman to our world today, I would conclude that she was of a liberal mindset, until she met Christ. Interestingly, Christ told her, "If you drink of me, you will never thirst again."

What we experience when we do things our own way is that the fantasy or expectation of a forever-satisfying experience or a future where our problems are resolved once and for all often turns out to be nothing. It's usually more like the high hopes and expectations that precede opening a vault on a live TV show, only to discover the vault is empty.

Arguably, if anyone would understand what it means to thirst, it should be this woman. She had lived through one marriage after another, looking for fulfillment but never finding it, moving on to the next person, and then the next, ... until she met Christ. John 4:1-42, there are three important things about this woman that made heaven locate her.

## Light in the Last Days

The first was that she acknowledged the ancient landmark when she argued with Christ about the greatness of Jacob, their forefather. She was proud to refer to herself as the daughter of Jacob. Secondly, the woman acknowledged her past life, which is the first step in getting heaven's attention. In verse 25, the woman said, "I know that Messiah" (called Christ) "is coming. When He comes, He will explain everything to us."

Thirdly, she knew she was a Samaritan, and that the coming Messiah would be from a Jewish background. Despite the Jews and the Samaritans having nothing in common, this woman was still looking forward to the coming of the Messiah. She was also open to what the Messiah had to say. This is an example of a harvest that is ripe.

Just like Ayaan Hirsi Ali, who was an acclaimed atheist and suffered bouts of depression, she was only able to overcome her deep feeling of emptiness after giving the Bible a try. There is a way out of depression, particularly where medical interventions have failed, and that way is the way of hope, the hope found in the word of God. There are numerous promises of hope and examples of people who have endured immense trials and difficulties, like Joseph, David, and many others mentioned in the Bible, who emerged victorious in the end. These things are written to encourage us, especially during our own trials, and to assure us of what God has said concerning us, knowing that this will surely come to pass.

Today, in the UK and across the world, many people have stopped watching the news. When asked why, they often say it leaves them feeling worse than before they tuned in. This constant stream of fear, anger, violence, grief, and death reflects the broken state of our world.

A powerful illustration of this is found in the book of Luke, chapter 7. In this passage, we see two contrasting groups: one is a procession of mourners leaving the city, grieving the death of a young boy. The other is a crowd full of life and hope, entering the city with Jesus at the centre.

This scene isn't suggesting that those walking with Jesus are exempt from pain or hardship. The difference lies in their perspective. They believe that Jesus has the power to change their circumstances. That hope changes everything.

It's important to recognize the real pain and sorrow of those who mourn. But what the story shows us is this, when Christ enters a situation, everything can change. The grief-stricken were not ignored they were met with compassion. And in an instant, their sorrow turned to joy.

God understands that the world we live in is a fallen world, filled with troubles that overwhelm many people. In times of hopelessness, like the kind we see in our world today, the Bible has become the go-to source where people can find hope. Hopelessness is often the result of fear about what the future holds.

One good example of God addressing our fears is in the bible book of Matthew 10:29-31 [NIV].

"29 Are not two sparrows sold for a penny? Yet not one of them will fall to the ground outside your Father's care.[a] 30 And even the very hairs of your head are all numbered. 31 So don't be afraid; you are worth more than many sparrows."

Considering the above verse, it means that if God would not allow the birds to die carelessly, despite being of much lesser worth to humans, then God will jealously guide and protect you. Of course, we rarely see birds falling from the sky and dying carelessly, except in the case of some incident. God is saying, "We are of much more value to Him than the birds, and if birds would not die carelessly, humans who are dearer to Him, will have a secure future."

Anyone overtaken by hopelessness will surely find hope in the Bible, though many have not yet taken the bold step to read the Bible, let alone meditate on God's promises.

When it comes to mental health, it is important to state that receiving treatment and undergoing therapy are also important. The wisdom of putting our hope in God in times of hopelessness does not negate the need for therapy. Let the doctors provide the treatment while God provides the healing. Although some Christians may choose not to seek medical intervention because they believe their faith can carry them, this does not apply to everyone. Therefore, those seeking therapy due to feelings of depression can receive therapy but should trust their healing in the hands of God.

The word "FEAR NOT" and phrases such as "do not be afraid" or even "be courageous," the positive way of telling us not to be afraid appear throughout the Bible. Imagine the reaction of the father of the prodigal son when he saw his son from afar. The way the father ran toward his son indicates that he had been worried about his son's well-being and had been looking forward to his return.

The prodigal son thought that returning to his father might be complicated and intended to ask for the place of a servant, but his father gave him the place of a son instead. God cares about our well-being, and it doesn't matter how many opportunities we may have squandered. What matters most to God is that we return to Him with a contrite heart while putting our hope in Him.

To gain better insight, I used a hypothetical situation to bring some illumination to Matthew 10:29-31. This was part of a recent conversation between my younger son and me during a Bible study.

I said, "Suppose he is on a bus returning home from school and hears people talking about the biting inflation, which means people are unable to afford groceries, and how empty the shelves are in the shops, just as they were during the COVID-19 pandemic." Unfortunately, this became the conversation every adult on the bus was having at the time, as some narrated their personal experiences. Interestingly, while this dreadful situation was being discussed, my teenager received a phone call from his mom, who told him she had just finished making two of his favorite dishes and was about to start making his favorite dessert.

Even though this teenager had not yet laid hands on the delicious meal waiting for him at home, his conversation with his mom provided hope, in contrast to the conversation happening around him. While my son would not dismiss the fact that the shelves are empty out there, his conversation with his mom represented hope that what was happening out there would not be his experience when he got home. In the same way, it doesn't matter what circumstances surround us, God is saying, "I've got your back."

It's clear that when you're going through tough times, every second of your life can feel like eternity. It's as if you're stuck in an endless loop, even though life keeps moving around you. Life's troubles can be overwhelming at times, yet God is saying, "You've got me. I am your reward. I will do this with you. Just trust me."

That's why Christ said not to worry about what tomorrow will bring. Christ's assurances aren't just empty words; He is saying, "I have already said yes to your request. Why are you still worrying?" He's re-emphasizing the heart of God so that we can enjoy God's peace. He is working behind the scenes, saying "yes" to our prayers, holding our hands, and catching us when necessary to ensure we don't fall.

# CHAPTER EIGHTEEN

*Staying in the presence of God*

Everything about the Christian faith is centered on our ability to have and maintain a relationship with God. Our relationship with God is not just limited to a brief walk with Him, but a lifelong journey. And journeying with God will not be possible without remaining in His presence. The problem we face as Christians is that many times, we profess a relationship with God, but our hearts and actions say otherwise. The children of Israel were in the presence of the Lord, but their hearts were in Egypt. That is why, at the slightest opportunity, they returned to worship the golden calf. The buzz and chattering of the crowd that filled the air as they worshipped the golden calf explain the joy they derived from having a taste of Egypt once again, even while in the presence of God.

Abraham's father, Terah, would have either had a God experience or become a distraction if he had followed his son, Abraham, to the land of Canaan, where God had called him.

Interestingly, just like many who, along the way, looked back to the comfort they once enjoyed, Terah began his journey with his son from the city of Ur, where they originally lived, but stopped at Haran because it resembled the city he had left behind—Ur.

Similarly, Lot's wife had escaped destruction. She was with the angels of God, but her heart was still in Sodom. Unfortunately, many times Christians incur the wrath of God when they align with those who are disobedient. They sometimes become collateral damage in a punishment they have already been saved from. Lot's wife was an example of this. Although she had escaped to safety, she aligned herself with Sodom and ended up incurring the fate of those in Sodom. She became a pillar of salt instead of being destroyed by brimstone.

The young rich ruler loves the salvation Christ offers, and he seems to want to go all in, but his heart lies in his wealth. We can know where our heart lies by our actions. Our actions and our words should speak the same thing, there must be no discordant tune when our words and actions are laid side by side.

The body of Esau but the voice of Jacob is something the world can easily spot. This is when we are Christians only by association, bodily, but our actions and personality say otherwise. The body of Esau and the voice of Jacob is more like the fig tree that attracted Christ, only for Christ to realize the tree had no fruit, which resulted in Jesus cursing the tree.

Matthew 21:18-19. "18 Early in the morning, as Jesus was on his way back to the city, he was hungry. 19 Seeing a fig tree by the road, he went up to it but found nothing on it except leaves. Then he said to it, "May you never bear fruit again!" Immediately the tree withered."

The story of Christ's reaction to the fig tree reinforces God's word that He hates lukewarm Christians. Christ's was the dispensation of grace, but that did not stop Him from showing His displeasure with the fig tree.

Partial obedience is disobedience, and that was what caused God to turn His back on King Saul (1 Samuel 15:14-23). He went to war as God instructed, but he did not carry out all of God's commands. The story of the young and old prophets is also another example (1 Kings 13:11-25). The young prophet made the journey to deliver God's prophecy but disobeyed God by going into the house of the old prophet.

It's obvious that we are in the dispensation of grace, and our disobedience may not always be met with a swift reaction from God, as in the case of King Saul and the young prophet. However, it is still of great importance to understand God's perception of partial obedience. As far as God is concerned, we are not an afterthought, nor are we like a fifth wheel in a car.

The book of Psalms, chapters 1-3, sheds more light on what is expected of us as Christians in order to meet the needs of our world today.

Psalm 1:1-3. NLT. "1 Oh, the joys of those who do not follow the advice of the wicked, or stand around with sinners, or join in with mockers. 2 But they delight in the law of the Lord, meditating on it day and night. 3 They are like trees planted along the river bank, bearing fruit each season. Their leaves never wither, and they prosper in all they do."

Let's pause for a moment as we consider a tree planted by the rivers of water, whose leaves are in season and out of season. This is a metaphor for people who are spiritually healthy, productive, and successful. One of the greatest insights into Psalms 1:1-3 was preached by Tony Wastall of Lifespring Church, when he said that the fruit of the apple tree is not enjoyed by the tree itself, but by others. If the tree is watered by virtue of its staying connected, it will bear fruit that provides nourishment to others.

As Christians, if God blesses us, then that blessing is not just for us to testify of God's goodness in our lives, rather, it is about God's grace in having found us worthy to be used as a channel of His blessings.

If we are the tree, then it would be right to say that the tree itself is just a channel of God's blessings to others. We are both financial and spiritual conduits. Just as a fruit tree does not eat its own fruit, we are not blessed financially or empowered with spiritual gifts just for our own consumption.

The parable in Luke 11:5-13 also shows us that the man going to knock on his friend's door at midnight to ask for bread, so he could entertain his friend who had come from a journey, was doing so because he needed to host his friend. This further reinforces the need to understand that the Christian journey isn't just about ourselves.

Let's ponder a story my father told me when I was very little. I don't know if this is a real-life story, but there is a lot of wisdom in it. It was a story about two friends who cared deeply for each other.

For the sake of context, let's refer to them as **Mr. A** and **Mr. B**. The love between these friends was such that they each put the other person's interests first, each worrying about how the other was coping with the limited resources at their disposal. It happened that Mr. A and Mr. B needed to share some goods between themselves. Mr. A had his own problems, almost as large as Mr. B's, but he was concerned that Mr. B's share of the goods might not be enough to meet his needs. Worried that Mr. B would object if he asked him to take the larger share of the goods, he decided to handle the matter differently. At midnight, Mr. A decided to take some of his own share of the goods, intending to add to his friend's portion. Interestingly, while Mr. A was on his way, carrying the goods to top up Mr. B's share, he stumbled into Mr. B, who was also carrying goods, heading to add to Mr. A's share.

*Light in the Last Days*

"What are you doing, and where are you going, with goods in your hands?" asked Mr. A.

"I was worried that your share of the goods wouldn't be enough to solve your problems, so I'm going to top up your share with some of mine," replied Mr. B.

"I was going to do the same! I wanted to top up your share with some of mine," Mr. A said. The friends hugged each other, as their friendship and care for each other were visibly evident.

This story of two friends sharing goods, with each of them going out at midnight to take some of their own share to top up the other person's share, is a story of people displaying acts of selflessness.

They were actively prioritizing the well-being of their friend over their own immediate needs by giving up part of their own portion.

This story, like some other Bible stories where God showed up, is about someone who is deeply interested in the welfare of the other person.

Arguably, before Christ was born, serving God was quite a ritual, requiring rigid protocols. We see in the Bible how priests would have bells around their waists so that people would know when the priest entered and exited the Holy of Holies. They usually had ropes tied to the priest in case he died in the Holy of Holies. Many believed the idea of the rope was to ensure that they could pull the priest out if he didn't make it out alive when he came before God. This rope became the only means to pull the priest out, because any man unauthorized by God going into the Holy of Holies to retrieve the priest would also not make it out alive. This whole system was too formal and rigid, and God needed to make our service to Him less cumbersome.

Christ did a great job of presenting God to us as someone relatable. When asked how we should pray, instead of referring to God with titles that show reverence, He presented God as a father. God has several titles, including Adonai, El-Shaddai, Yahweh, Elohim, Ebenezer, Omnipotent, Omnipresent, and many others. These titles place God in a league far beyond the human level. Yet Christ used the word "Father" to describe how we should relate to God. He tore the temple curtain in two to grant access to everyone, and He now referred to God as Father, which highlights God's deliberate move to change His relationship with humans through Christ.

So, God decided to deny Himself the pleasure of having His Son around for 33 years, just to make His relationship with humans less rigid. God Himself demonstrated this selflessness beforehand. He gave up His Son for the benefit of mankind. Christ Himself did not hold back, He left the glory of heaven, where He was being worshiped, and stepped into a world of scarcity and pain.

Christ was born to a carpenter who worked with wood. He was likely injured by nails and may have had His hand pierced by a piece of wood. He must have sweated while working with wood under the heat of the sun alongside His father, Joseph. He may have built benches and tables for people, or perhaps taken them to the marketplace for people to buy.

Christ was not born into a royal home where everything would be done for Him. Rather, He was born into the home of a carpenter, where He would experience a humble beginning. He suffered hunger, fasted, and felt fatigued. While people were asleep, He was mostly on boats at sea, experiencing the worst sea conditions. He walked on foot, traveling every nook and cranny of Israel mostly on foot before facing an excruciating death. This was what God allowed His Son, the Jewel of Heaven and the Spoken Word of Creation, to endure. God did all of this for us.

Christ knew that His disciples would betray, deny, and desert Him. He was aware that even His Father in heaven would turn His face away as the sins of the world were laid upon Him. Despite this foreknowledge, as He sat with His disciples during the Last Supper, breaking bread with them, He remained composed and resolute.

Christ knew beforehand what He was getting into, and He did not hold back. After all, He had visited the earth several times before He was officially born. He showed up in the fiery furnace alongside the three Hebrew children, and He also appeared as Melchizedek. He knew what the world He was coming into looked like, and yet He did not hold back. He went all the way to the cross, where He paid the ultimate sacrifice. This story is about sacrificing for the sake of others.

The entire story of salvation is about the other person, and what attracts God the most are sacrifices made for others to the glory of God. This is what staying in the presence of God means. This does not take away the fact that when we ourselves are in need and call on God, He will show up. Job prayed for his friends, and God restored him. Even in the midst of his troubles, Job trusted God, but he focused too much on his problems. He moved God into immediate action the moment he focused on his friends and prayed for them. David's decision to take on Goliath wasn't out of personal ego, but about defending the honor of God and His people..

Goliath's defiance was an affront to God's authority, and that was something David found too hard to stomach. God is more interested in using you as a point of blessing or hope for someone believing or trusting God to come through for them. As mentioned earlier, the apple tree does not eat its fruit, rather, the fruit is to the benefit of others. As Christians, we are trees planted by the rivers of water, and our water is Christ. Let's produce fruit that benefits others.

It means our good nature, our wealth, and every fruit of the Spirit manifested in our lives should be for the benefit of others. This is important, particularly to show forth the glory of God in a manner that, as people enjoy our fruits, they should attest to the goodness of God and be drawn to His light in our lives.

Moreover, it is expected that while this tree remains connected to its source of water, its leaves will be green and flourishing, providing shade for those seeking comfort.

In Psalm 23, when David mentions his "cup running over" (Psalm 23:5), he is expressing a sense of abundance and overflowing blessings. It suggests that God's provision is not only sufficient for David's own needs but also abundant enough to share with others. The image of an overflowing cup symbolizes the generosity and grace of God, which goes beyond mere sufficiency, offering more than enough to bless both the individual and those around them.

## Light in the Last Days

It is, therefore, important to note that as Christians, fellow believers should find us to be peaceable. Being controversial and always wanting to have the last word does not align with the tree described in Psalm 1–3, which is meant to provide comfort.

Every miracle Christ performed was to showcase the glory of God. Christ emphasized that His miracle of raising Lazarus from the dead was to demonstrate the glory of God. Therefore, being controversial and unbearable as a person defeats the purpose of the fruit of the Spirit, as these fruits are meant to benefit others.

A growing concern in our world today is that many people fall back into their former lifestyles after experiencing a powerful encounter with the Holy Spirit during a revival. This often happens due to a lack of proper discipleship.

A true revival drives out darkness and brings the light of Christ. But for that light to endure, we must rely on the Holy Spirit. Without His strong guidance, the enemy will inevitably return, like a steady IV drip, trying to revive the very darkness that was cast out. This is often what causes revivals to fade. That's why it's essential to pursue lasting reformation once revival has begun.

As Christians, we can no longer be content with cities and nations filled with mega-churches, where God's Word is preached in every corner and people regularly fall under the anointing, while ungodliness continues to prevail at alarming levels in those same places.

In response, many churches involved in revival movements across nations are shifting their focus, not just seeking revival, but also pursuing reformation. While revival sparks a fresh encounter with the Holy Spirit, reformation ensures that new believers are nurtured through intentional discipleship. This combination helps them become firmly rooted in their faith and empowered to live godly lives.

Therefore, for reformation to truly take root, our lives as priests, pastors, evangelists, and believers must embody the message we preach, demonstrating the fruit of the Spirit. Without a transformed heart, the effects of revival will be short-lived.

It is understandable that we cannot give what we don't have. Our idea of God's goodness should not only be about how much of it is reflected in our lives, rather, it should be about the extent to which others benefit from God's goodness in our lives.

As Christians, we are called to bear fruit consistently, both in season and out of season. Even when no one seems to be partaking of what we offer, we must continue to produce fruit so that when someone turns to us unexpectedly, they will find it ready. Let us not be like the fig tree in Matthew 21:18–21, found barren when it was needed most.

Sometimes, even among believers, there is the tendency for one person to think they are more gifted or spiritual than others, which could lead to undermining other members of the body. The virtues of holiness and spirituality are key in our relationship with God, but God despises pride. We are meant to complement each other as different parts of the body, instead of fighting amongst ourselves. Apostle Paul also admonished the church about the need to work together in unity and complement each other.

1 Corinthians 3:6: "6 I have planted, Apollos watered; but God gave the increase." This implies that we are not in competition, but rather, we are to complement each other. Those with such a mindset are at risk of falling into the sin of pride. You can be holy, very dedicated, and perform many miracles, and yet still be guilty of the sin of pride.

Divisive Christians, no matter their understanding of the Bible or their faith in God, are destructive to the body of Christ. They win one soul but chase two people away from the congregation due to their character. They win two souls but chase five people away. They are even more destructive when in board positions in the church, as they often claim to have received negative revelations about others.

In John 15:1–17, Jesus describes Himself as the true vine and calls us the branches. Much of the focus is often on our responsibility to remain connected to Him. However, verses 1–2 reveal something sobering: it is God the Father who cuts off branches that do not bear fruit. This means it's possible to believe we are still connected to Christ, while in reality, we've already been cut off, and not even realize it.

That's why self-examination is so important. We must regularly measure our actions and lifestyle against the Word of God to ensure we are truly abiding in Christ. Because while we might not immediately notice when that connection is lost, the world often does. People can tell when our lives no longer reflect the faith we claim to live by.

My father once told me a story that illustrates this point well. A king and his slave were traveling to visit another king in a distant village. Before they arrived, the slave asked his master to present him as a friend rather than a slave so he would be treated with more respect. The king agreed.

On the way, heavy rain soaked them. Upon arrival, they changed clothes, and their host hung the wet garments out to dry. Later, the slave saw his clothes on the line and took them to the fireplace to dry them more quickly. As he did, the host's wife passed by, saw the garments by the fire, and without knowing whose they were, asked, "Whose slave owns these clothes?"

The slave quickly stepped forward and claimed them. His master looked at him silently, with a knowing expression that said, "You just exposed yourself." Despite being introduced as a friend, his actions betrayed his true position. His behaviour gave him away.

Likewise, you can't live like the world and still claim to represent Christ. Even those outside the faith can often tell when someone's actions don't align with their confession. Just like the slave, it's not your title that speaks the loudest; it's your conduct.

The popular philosopher and civil rights leader Mahatma Gandhi once said, "I like your Christ, I do not like your Christians..." He said this from his personal experience following his visit to a church. As Christians, it is important for us to understand that we are representatives of Christ here on earth. Therefore, the world should see Christ when they see us. They must have heard a lot of nice things about Christ, and that is what they expect to see when they come in contact with us.

Many unbelievers try to confuse God by describing Him from two different perspectives: firstly, from the perspective of the God in the Old Testament, and then the God in the New Testament. For some, the God in the Old Testament can't be the same as the loving God in the New Testament. Excessive focus on trying to marry the character of God in the Old Testament with the character of God through Christ in the New Testament might leave us questioning the personality of God, which will not do us any good. God has unveiled Christ, and therefore, our focus should be Christ and nothing else, because He has already paid the price for our sins.

I was watching a movie about a relationship between a former female stripper and a murderer who had just finished serving his jail term. They both found Christ and are now planning to get married. That movie kind of resonates with what being a new creation in Christ really means. Will Christ be a part of their new home? Of course, yes. Will they bear the consequences, if any, from the mistakes of their past lifestyle? Possibly, yes.

We might want to ponder how God addresses moral issues like forgiveness, mercy, and justice. Is it forgiveness at the expense of justice, or justice at the expense of mercy? One thing is certain, if we receive Christ into our lives, it is no longer about justice but about mercy and forgiveness.

When we remain in the presence of God by staying connected to the throne of grace, we will enjoy fresh mercies every day that will bring about a renewal of strength. I was listening to Dave Ramsey from EntreLeadership, and he said, "In the military, they have a saying: don't let the fighting lines, the men and women on the front line doing the fighting, advance past the supply. Gasoline, bullets, and food have to get to the front lines. If the front lines advance faster than the supply lines, where gasoline, bullets, and food can get to them, then the fighting men get killed." This is because they don't have the supplies to sustain them. This also applies to our Christian journey.

Going into things God has not called us to, particularly when it comes to ministry, might seem like having zeal for God, but the truth is that you are no longer relying on God for direction and sustenance. In some cases, God might pull you back to the path He has called you to, and in other cases, He will leave you to do your own thing until you run out of steam.

It is important to note that, irrespective of your area of calling in ministry, we have all been called to preach the good news of Christ. Just as it can be assumed in the military that advancing faster than the supplies is an indication that the fighting men are doing well, taking more territory and conquering the enemy, the truth remains that they are cut off from their source of sustenance.

Aside from what God has called us into, the best thing that can ever happen to any human as they sojourn on earth is to have God. We can do this by simply praying to God and reading His Word. When we pray, we are talking to God, but when we read the Bible, God is talking to us. Sojourning on this earth without God is no different from the front lines advancing faster than the supplies.

Someone once said, "If you have God, then you have everything," and that is true. If God is determined to keep you safe, then your safety is guaranteed. If it is your sustenance that you are concerned about, God is able to sustain you. God's provision did not stop with the manna from heaven while the Israelites were in the wilderness. When the Israelites requested meat, God sent the quail as a demonstration of His power to provide for their needs.

Imagine Elijah at the Brook Cherith during a famine and how God used ravens to bring bread and meat to Elijah twice a day while he was camping by the brook.

Some might be tempted to think that these stories of God's miraculous provision are only limited to Bible days, but this is not the case. Take, for example, the story of George Mueller and his orphanages built by prayer. Below is just one of the many miracles associated with George Mueller and his orphanage:

"The kids are dressed and prepared for school. However, there is no food available for them," the housemother of the orphanage told George Mueller. George instructed her to take the 300 children to the dining room and have them sit at the tables. He expressed his gratitude to God for the food and waited. George was confident that God would supply food for the children, as He had always done. Moments later, a baker knocked on the door. "Mr. Mueller," he said, "I couldn't sleep last night. I had a feeling you would need bread this morning, so I got up and baked three batches for you. I'll bring it in."

Before long, there was another tap on the door. It turned out to be the milkman. His cart had malfunctioned right in front of the orphanage. The milk would go bad before the wheel could be repaired. He inquired if George could spare some milk for free. George grinned as the milkman carried in ten sizable cans of milk. It was precisely the right amount for the 300 thirsty kids.

Staying connected would require total and unquestioning obedience where having God alone would be enough for us. John 2:5 "But his mother told the servants, "Do whatever he tells you." Mary advised the men at the marriage to do whatever Christ asks of them, this statement does not leave room for human rationalisation. It did not allow the men to question why Christ decided to go for the old and possibly rusty water pots and why the content should have been tested before serving it to the master of the ceremony. Provided it is God speaking, and not men telling you what you ought to be doing, then your connection is secured.

# CHAPTER NINETEEN

## *Walking with God*

Walking with God, in every sense, means stepping out of our comfort zone. It's about what God wants, not what we want. From Noah to Abraham, Moses, Jonah, and Paul, we see people leaving behind the lives they knew and stepping away from what they believed to be safe zones, into the unknown. God will never let you down in this partnership. He will order your steps, give you insight into what is expected of you, and uphold you as the journey continues. Many find it terrifying to go all in on their walk with God, especially in a world increasingly hostile to the Christian faith. When we focus on the turbulence that might come our way, the walk of faith becomes hindered. It's like someone being afraid of the thorns on a rose, forgetting the beauty and value of the rose itself.

Hebrews 11:4 speaks of faith: "By faith, Abel offered unto God a more excellent sacrifice than Cain. By faith, Noah, being warned by God of things not yet seen, moved with fear. By faith, Abraham, when he was called to go out into a place he would later receive as an inheritance ..." And Hebrews 11:39 [NIV] says: "These were all commended for their faith, yet none of them received what had been promised."

## Light in the Last Days

When Christ asked His disciples to go over to Galilee, the journey wasn't without danger. In fact, they had one of the most terrifying experiences of their lives. As they screamed in fear amidst the storm, they forgot that Christ was in their boat. The chaos, the fear, and the storm all ceased the moment Christ stepped in and took over.

Brethren, I want you to know, you are not alone. Christ is in your boat, just invite Him into the storm and watch what He does with it. The truth is, God is constantly knocking at the door of our hearts, but He won't knock forever. If we keep resisting Him, at some point, He'll leave us to our desires. God said He will spit out those who are neither hot nor cold. He would rather have believers who are fully for Him, or even an unbeliever like the Samaritan woman, whom He can pursue and win over.

In Luke 8:43-48, we see that God wants to know where we truly stand. We shouldn't be like the crowd thronging around Him and touching Him, yet feeling nothing from their closeness. This shows that the crowd was with Him physically, but not connected to Him spiritually. Every man desires a mountain-top experience with God, but in most cases, just like Lot, we'd rather stay in the valley than take the required step of faith. Valleys represent temporary comfort, they represent the known, as opposed to leaping into the unknown. They can also symbolize a place of contention with God. Let's now consider some examples of how staying in the valley can impact destiny.

Abraham's journey with God was stalled because he tied himself to his father. Just like in Abraham's case, it is understandable that we all find comfort with our families and loved ones.

However, prioritising comfort over our walk with God might mean that our life's purpose will not be realised. The children of Israel preferred to remain in the wilderness, enjoying the temporary comfort available to them, rather than cross the Jordan River to confront the children of Anak and move forward in their march toward destiny.

Lot also chose to remain in the plain of Sodom, a place he was familiar with and knew well, rather than escape to the mountains. Climbing a mountain is an arduous task and requires effort, but the mountain-top itself is a place of fulfilment. In the above three cases and in many other examples from the Bible, including our personal experiences, we can conclude that while avoiding a leap into the unknown may offer temporary comfort, destinies are often stalled or even destroyed in the end.

New believers can sometimes find their walk with God frustrating, especially when it feels like they're talking to someone who doesn't talk back. The Christian faith operates by faith, you do not see, yet you believe. The same faith applies when we pray to God.

You relate to God with the mindset that He is right beside you and that He hears you. All that is required is to open your mouth and speak to Him, He is listening. You can be confident that you are speaking to heaven as long as you continue to approach God humbly and persistently.

Luke 11:5-13. "5 Then Jesus said to them, "Suppose you have a friend, and you go to him at midnight and say, 'Friend, lend me three loaves of bread; 6 a friend of mine on a journey has come to me, and I have no food to offer him.' 7 And suppose the one inside answers, 'Don't bother me. The door is already locked, and my children and I are in bed. I can't get up and give you anything.' 8 I tell you, even though he will not get up and give you the bread because of friendship, yet because of your shameless audacity[a] he will surely get up and give you as much as you need.

9 "So I say to you: Ask and it will be given to you; seek and you will find; knock and the door will be opened to you. 10 For everyone who asks receives; the one who seeks finds; and to the one who knocks, the door will be opened.

11 "Which of you fathers, if your son asks for[b] a fish, will give him a snake instead? 12 Or if he asks for an egg, will give him a scorpion? 13 If you then, though you are evil, know how to give good gifts to your children, how much more will your Father in heaven give the Holy Spirit to those who ask him!"

Christ made us understand through the parable that we must be persistent in the place of prayer, because prayer cannot be a part-time commitment. Pastor John Blackah of Lifespring Church gave further illumination to this story by stating that the bread mentioned in the parable represents Christ Himself. While much focus has been placed on the importance of persistence in prayer, the content, bread, has not received as much attention. Christ Himself said, "I am the Bread of Life." During the Last Supper,

Jesus broke bread and gave it to His disciples, saying, "Take and eat; this is my body" (Matthew 26:26).

The Bible also tells us that bread was kept in the Temple of Jerusalem to represent God's presence. This has been interpreted to mean, the bread was a symbolic acknowledgment that God was the source of life and nourishment for Israel (Exodus 25:30). In the Bible verse John 10:10, Christ said, "I came that they might have life, and that they might have it more abundantly."

This also reinforces Christ as the source of life, symbolized by the bread in the temple. The fact that the man in the parable went as far as knocking on someone else's door at midnight just to get bread for a friend shows how far Christ expects us to go in helping others find Him.

The truth remains that God is responding, but He chooses how He responds to our prayers. What matters most is whether we are truly listening to what He is saying or if our spiritual eyes are clear enough to see what He is showing us. He speaks to us through the Bible, through the preacher on the pulpit, and through dreams. He also speaks through our conversations with others, sometimes as confirmation, or even through conversations between other people. Some people are taken into trances where God reveals things to them. God's response can sometimes be very direct, like when you misplace something and, after searching for it for weeks, you finally decide to pray. Then, within hours, you suddenly stumble upon it. In other cases, His response is immediate and clear, but it still requires spiritual discernment. For instance, David inquired of the Lord and received an instant reply, God told him to pursue, and assured him that he would recover all.

I have seen God's immediate response in action in my life, but one of the most striking confirmations of God's response happened years ago when my elder brother, after being jobless for a while, decided to go on a three-day fast. On the third day, at the end of the fast, he picked up a Christian book with hundreds of pages. As he opened it to scan through the content, the subheading on the page he stumbled into, reads, "Now that you have gotten a job." This book covered a wide range of topics and wasn't specifically about employment, but God led him to a page that directly addressed his prayer. Within two weeks, my brother received an invitation for an interview, and less than a month after getting that confirmation through the book, he was offered a job.

Of course, this isn't always the case, God's response can also be subtle, following a "wait and see" approach. That doesn't take away the fact that God may also be silent at times, which could mean that the timing isn't right, or that it's simply not part of His plan for us. Our walk with God requires two key ingredients: the first is faith, and the second is obedience. These must be complemented by two primary gifts that act as the vehicles of the Christian faith.

The two most precious gifts to mankind are Christ and the Holy Spirit. What makes Christ a gift to humanity is clarified in John 3:16: "For God so loved the world, that He gave His only Son, that whoever believes in Him should not perish but have eternal life." A gift is defined as something given willingly to someone without payment. Considering this definition, and the fact that God gave His Son willingly when we did not deserve it, we can rightly conclude that Christ is indeed a gift.

The second gift is the Holy Spirit, given to empower believers. The gift of Jesus Christ is for our personal salvation, while the gift of the Holy Spirit is given to equip us to reach others. Christ came to reconcile us to God; the Holy Spirit was sent to guide our walk with God and to empower us in advancing His Kingdom.

Acts 2:3-4 says, "They saw what seemed to be tongues of fire that separated and came to rest on each of them. All of them were filled with the Holy Spirit and began to speak in other tongues as the Spirit enabled them." The disciples had waited in the upper room after Christ's ascension, not to receive Christ again, but to be empowered to reach others.

The Bible records that on that same day, three thousand people believed and were baptized. This shows that the work of the Holy Spirit goes beyond personal benefit, it is meant to produce fruit that impacts the lives of others. The fact that our earthly journey does not end the moment we give our lives to Christ indicates our need for the Holy Spirit to guide us, direct us, and manifest the fruit of the Spirit through us for the benefit of others.

A walk with God requires spiritual insight, and this insight is cultivated through our connection with the Spirit. One of the biggest questions we must each answer is, If we saw God, would we recognize Him? Abraham did, he saw God from afar and ran to meet Him. He recognized the divine presence in the form of three men, one being God and the other two angels, as he sat at the entrance of his tent.

Insight and the ability to discern are essential in our walk with God. Abraham and Lot were able to exercise discernment correctly because they knew things about God that others did not. If you don't know God, how will you recognize Him, or His angels when they walk past you looking just like an ordinary person on your street?

Genesis 18:1-5 [NIV]. "The Lord appeared to Abraham near the great trees of Mamre while he was sitting at the entrance to his tent in the heat of the day. 2 Abraham looked up and saw three men standing nearby. When he saw them, he hurried from the entrance of his tent to meet them and bowed low to the ground. 3 He said, "If I have found favor in your eyes, my lord,[a] do not pass your servant by. 4 Let a little water be brought, and then you may all wash your feet and rest under this tree. 5 Let me get you something to eat, so you can be refreshed and then go on your way—now that you have come to your servant." "Very well," they answered, "do as you say."

*Light in the Last Days*

The question remains, how did Abraham know the person he saw from afar is God.

In like manner, Lot saw the angels and immediately reached out to them deliberately.

19:1-5 [NIV]. The two angels arrived at Sodom in the evening, and Lot was sitting in the gateway of the city. When he saw them, he got up to meet them and bowed down with his face to the ground. 2 "My lords," he said, "please turn aside to your servant's house. You can wash your feet and spend the night and then go on your way early in the morning."

"No," they answered, "we will spend the night in the square."

3 But he insisted so strongly that they did go with him and entered his house. He prepared a meal for them, baking bread without yeast, and they ate. 4 Before they had gone to bed, all the men from every part of the city of Sodom—both young and old—surrounded the house. 5 They called Lot, "Where are the men who came to you tonight? Bring them out to us so that we can have sex with them."

What virtue did Abraham pass to Lot that made him see what other men by the gate missed about these men being angels.

It is common knowledge that Lot made some poor choices, choosing to stay in the valley of Sodom rather than on the mountain top where the angels had originally intended for him to go. However, this does not take away from the fact that Lot had insight the people of Sodom did not possess. Ultimately, walking with God requires intentionality and a sense of responsibility.

We see a similarity in how both Abraham and Lot approached God and the angels. They didn't just look at them from a distance and say, "Oh, that looks like an angel," or "That might be God," and then simply watch as He passed by. Instead, they acted. They approached and pleaded to be their hosts. Abraham didn't even tell

Lot that the angels were on their way to Sodom; Lot responded personally and on his own initiative.

As Christians, we cannot afford to be nonchalant. We must be willing to take responsibility for Christ and for our faith. Don't say, "As long as I'm serving my God, what happens out there is not my concern." That mindset contradicts the very heart of the gospel.

# CHAPTER TWENTY

## *Progressive Liberalism to a Dead End*

The definition of being "progressive" is often framed in the context of pleasure, pursuing happiness to satisfy one's desires. In most cases, these "progressives," who engage in all manner of pleasure to make themselves happy, do indeed find some happiness in it. However, this happiness does not endure. Because the expectation of lasting happiness is not met, they often feel hollow and become the loneliest people, bored and tired of life, with many even attempting suicide.

Many of these progressives are tech-savvy, with all manner of electronic gadgets meant to produce pleasure, yet they remain bored and lonely. You will notice that most of the adults and children who engage in self-harm are often those exposed to everything society offers. They have access to good phones, iPads, laptops, and parents who give them whatever they ask for. They engage fully in social networks, trying to make themselves happy and fulfilled. Yet, they are still bored and tired of life, with some resorting to self-harm as an attempt to "sign out" of life. This is because there is nothing in the world that satisfies the void and curiosity in their hearts, and they remain unhappy. At this point, they blame their life woes on any available excuse they can find.

Unfortunately, the lifestyle that the so-called progressives seek often leads to a dead end. You'll realize that the more a person engages in perverse sexual acts, the less satisfying sex becomes. This leads to a progression where the individual moves from having sex with one person to engaging in multiple partners through hedonistic sex parties, as the pleasure continues to diminish. The more they chase this "new level of pleasure," the less fulfilling it becomes.

Take marriage, for example. You'll find that those who have divorced their spouse simply because they "fell out of love" and for no other reason, often have a higher tendency to divorce again and again. This is because relationships become less satisfying over time. Anyone living a life without God and professing happiness is living a lie, it's like someone lying on a bed of nails and telling everyone, "It's so comfy."

What was once considered bad by societal values for hundreds of years is now seen as good, and what was once considered a good value or standard norm is now regarded as bad. Efforts to suppress the Christian faith have largely failed, and in order to achieve this, the word of God is now deemed "hate speech."

Society is now being divided into heroes and villains, good guys and bad guys, as progressives try to force their understanding of truth onto society as a whole. In all our endeavors in life, it is a well-known fact that every human organization is guided by a set of rules, whether it be in the university environment, the workplace, the home, the club, the church, the schools, or even the marketplace.

Aside from poor mental health, some people are naturally chaotic, perhaps due to their upbringing or because they chose to live on the edge. Instead of getting their act together, chaotic people, who cannot manage their lives properly, often assume the posture of a liberal by claiming to be victimized. They then seek to force their unguarded lifestyle onto the larger population as the way forward, after all, they are the victims, and everyone else must sympathize with them. Pastor Femi Lazarus once said, "You have no reason to be offended at anybody for the foolishness you began." Instead of society accommodating such individuals by making room for them to get their lives back on track, liberals now want their lifestyle to become the lifestyle of the entire society.

The home is where a person's character is formed, and this is achieved through a stable marriage and a stable home. Marriage is ordained by God, but unfortunately, marriage is now seen as something mundane. It is understandable that many have tried marriage, given it their all, but things didn't work out. However, this does not suddenly make marriage something to be sneered at, because God's original plan is for children to grow under the care of their biological parents—and it still is. A quote from Candace Owens, "The government has removed the sacred from the home in so many ways," explains the rapid decline in our quality of life. Seeing how children are left with hopelessness following a family breakdown is often too distressing for words.

The same governments that have contributed to family breakdowns now attempt to create a semblance of normalcy for children. Yet, their efforts have failed to replace God's original design, for children to be raised by their biological parents.

Liberalism has been weaponized to mean a total dismantling of common sense and established values. Unfortunately, it is now clear that progressives are particularly focused on bringing down the Christian faith among all other faiths. There is no other reason for this except that these so-called progressives are afraid of the truth, and that truth lies only in the Christian faith. They pay less attention to other faiths, why bother with other faiths that lack the potency of the Christian faith?

In the name of political correctness, progressives are quick to attack the Christian view that "only true believing Christians will make heaven." They consider it absolutism because the Christian view emphasizes moderation in our actions and does not accommodate any other view outside of "putting our faith wholly in Christ and His teachings." If Christians are accused of absolutism for not accommodating contrary views, why then should progressives become agitated whenever a Christian expresses a view contrary to theirs? Progressives are now taking the posture of absolutism, which they accuse Christians of, if they cannot accommodate any contrary view outside of their own.

These so-called progressives employ the tool of collective rights, working in unison, with their central focus being to bring down established societal norms and common sense. Collective rights is a posture in which, when one individual is offended, everyone is supposedly offended, even though the so-called offense has not been justified. Collective rights can be likened to totalitarianism and is usually enforced through the state in the form of political correctness. Most political correctness is the result of collective rights, even when it is devoid of common sense.

Progressives typically pursue liberalism by working hand-in-hand with neoliberal media that suppresses the "Christian truth" while spreading the lies and fantasies behind the values of progressive liberalism. They do this by projecting fake news. However, fake news here does not mean a total absence of truth. These media outlets project news that contains some elements of truth, but is laced with deception that twists the entire narrative into something fake, though presented to viewers and readers as genuine and truthful.

The move by some leading churches in Western society in recent years to push for secularity has done nothing but increase the drumbeat against the need for God in our daily lives. Recent efforts by the Church of England to drop the word "church" and replace it with the word "community" is another example of the church cheerleading secularity in the Western hemisphere. This might seem like a non-essential doctrinal issue with no consequence in our relationship with Christ, but it matters if the goal is to move the church toward secularity. More importantly, this move aims to strip away the peculiarity of Christian gatherings, making them resemble the gatherings of the world. This is not about the church being welcoming to all, rather, it is a way of allowing the church to lose its saltiness and look more like the world. As Dr. Pastor Paul Enenche once said, "You cannot make a difference in the people until you are different from them, the impact is in the difference" (Acts 5:13-14).

In Matthew 16:11, Jesus cautioned His disciples to "beware of the yeast of the Pharisees and Sadducees." He wasn't referring to bread, but rather to their deceptive teachings and hypocrisy. In Jewish tradition, yeast (or leaven) symbolized corruption, decay, and evil influence. Furthermore, yeast in the context of bread means that the bread is neither entirely yeast nor entirely flour. Similarly, when Jesus mentioned yeast, He was referring to the actions of the Pharisees and the distorted message they preached, despite claiming to be custodians of the word of God. Here, Christ is warning us to be cautious of any preacher of the gospel whose message has been corrupted, leading people astray from God's truth.

The church's subtle use of beautiful phrases that downplay their intention to dilute the Christian faith is like changing the horse but keeping the same jockey, the destination remains the same. Many liberals have consistently offered faint praise to the leaders of the Church of England for their push to move the church towards secularism.

Let's not be deceived, erasing God's morals is the main objective of all these maneuvers. A church where God does not have the final say, but the people do, is what the Church has turned into. Disguising these moves with enough lipstick does not make what God called bad suddenly become good. The pride of life and the arrogance surrounding this move may seem grand from the fist-pump standpoint, but in the end, God will still have the final say.

Unfortunately, the Church of England is emptying out right before our eyes, and it is emptying out quickly as members leave in droves. Many of the church buildings have been purchased and are now being used as mosques, Sikh temples, and even pubs. Even those they intend to win into the church are not interested. They can see through the gymnastics and can clearly discern that this church can no longer help them find the peace, hope, and reconciliation that Christ offers.

If we think the world, with whom the church seeks to please, does not know the difference between a spirit-led and a secular-led church doctrine, then how come King Nebuchadnezzar, a heathen king, knew that the fourth person in the midst of the fire alongside the three Hebrew children was like the Son of God?

Acts 19:15-16 [NIV]: 15 "And the evil spirit answered and said, 'Jesus I know, and Paul I know; but who are you?' 16 Then the man in whom the evil spirit was leaped on them, overpowered them, and prevailed against them, so that they fled out of that house naked and wounded." The Spirit of God bears witness with the truth, and even a madman knows when the Spirit of God is at work.

Moreover, while many people are eager to drop that aspect of their history because they now see the Christian faith as a game of musical chairs that needs to be quickly abandoned, some are embracing it wholeheartedly. To be fair, it is important to avoid painting all the priests of the Church of England with a broad brush. There are plenty of priests who still hold dearly to their orthodox view of the Bible. They continue to uphold the true teachings of Christ. These contrasting views have caused a significant division within the Church of England.

Arguably, priests aren't politicians. While politicians are meant to represent the views and values of their constituents, priests are meant to tell the people the mind of God, irrespective of how hard the truth may be. However, the fact that a word is from God does not necessarily mean we should throw wisdom and common sense away when delivering it. Remember the saying, "There is no point giving a man a rose to smell after you've cut off his nose."

Many must be used to the frowns and anger that the Christian faith attracts, even as the world tolerates other religions. As Christians, we can't just be passive in today's world. Imagine a large dining table filled with guests around it, and there is a pile of garbage in the middle of the table. No one can eat with this garbage in the middle of the table. Everyone is looking at the garbage and expecting someone to remove it, but no one is making the move to take it out so they can eat comfortably.

Sometimes we live a quiet and peaceful life and would rather not get involved in shaking the tree. Unfortunately, shaking the tree is what we have been called to do. The word of God is light, and just the presence of light alone upsets darkness. Even before Christ attempted to cast out the demons, His presence alone made the demons inside the madman of Gadara uncomfortable. That is what shaking the tree looks like. If we carry the light of God, the status quo will not remain the same the moment we walk into a place. The gospel does not leave people the same, it does unimaginable things to people on the inside because it shows you who you really are. That is what the devil is afraid of, the darkness in our lives wants to stay hidden while still doing damage and will protest against anything exposing that darkness to us.

We must remember that we will have to steel our spines the moment we carry our cross. This is because the word of God will surely offend some people, no matter how nicely it is presented. There will be backlash against you at times, but many will also come back to thank you for daring to bring them the word, because it came at the nick of time, when they needed it most.

Some Christians have assumed the position of a mud monster when dealing with people with extreme liberal values who have issues with every single word of God, notwithstanding how nicely or humbly it is presented. They throw mud at Christians at the slightest opportunity. Throwing mud at them no longer bothers them, they just go on preaching the good news to reach those who are ripe for harvest. The persecution of Christians is not something new. It has been present since the time of Christ but has not stopped the good news. A genuine Christian would walk across broken glass to make sure the church of God marches on. Christ suffered the same at the hands of the Pharisees and Sadducees. He got used to their hypocrisy and went about doing the work of His Father.

Without courage, we will end up as people with good ideas that were never acted upon. Wayne Gretzky was right when he said, "You miss 100% of the shots you don't take." The Bible describes a person without Christ as lost, which is the underlying message in the parable of the lost sheep. Unfortunately, lost people often don't realize they are lost. How we engage with them in debates about God requires an understanding that they perceive Christ as a savior differently.

As Christians, it is important to understand that not all harvests are ripe, but we must start with the mindset that the harvest before us is ripe for God until the Holy Spirit ministers otherwise. However, we should not get bogged down by unripe harvests and, in doing so, miss the souls that are ripe for the harvest. Christ knew that the people in His hometown were not ripe, as were the Pharisees. He did not do much to convince them because He knew they were not ripe for the harvest.

We are to show Christ's love to all, including non-Christians and even those who are avidly against Christians. Therefore, it is important that we do not quickly assume that those who backlash against Christians are not ripe for the harvest and belong to padded cells.

Rather, we should hear their concerns about God and help them see the Light in the Word by sharing God's goodness with them.

In the secular world, I was taught that a complaining customer can sometimes end up becoming an advocate or a partner of the firm. Some customers seek good service and their desire for integrity, honesty, and quality can make them appear demanding in a way that service providers may mistakenly perceive them as merely complaining. Research has shown that firms that take the time to address the concerns of these customers often win them over. This is because these customers are outspoken, never shy to advocate for the firm, and some even end up becoming partners. The most important thing here is our perception of the customer. If we perceive a customer as a problem, our desire to address their concerns and satisfy them will be hindered. But when we perceive the customer as a potential advocate for the firm, we will gladly make the effort to address their concerns.

In the same vein, as Christians, our goal should not be to win the argument. Christ Himself did not expect His disciples to engage in arguments when He sent them out. Our responsibility is to present Christ in the best possible way, in a manner that exudes love.

Let's not be like the priest and the Levite in the story of the Good Samaritan, who claimed to be God's people but did not show the love of Christ when it was needed most. Matthew 10:14: "If anyone will not welcome you or listen to your words, leave that home or town and shake the dust off your feet."

There are several interpretations of this verse. While some interpret the dusting of our sandals as the earth bearing witness that the good news has been preached, others interpret it as a reminder not to force the good news of Christ onto unwilling hearts.

In truth, people whom we consider antagonists to the Christian faith might end up becoming men of God, particularly where God has a plan for such a soul. There are several examples in the Bible and even in our world today where people who have persecuted Christians physically or spiritually ended up becoming Christians. We should, therefore, not be too quick to conclude that a person's heart is not ripe for the good news after meeting them for the first time. We should be patient with people who are hostile and antagonistic toward the Christian faith, and rather continue to pray for God to reveal Himself to them, as they might become strong advocates of the faith.

Moreover, as Christians, we are not in a position to conclude who God is capable of using, because the ways of God are different from ours. Many are quick to accuse Christians of hypocrisy, possibly because some are still struggling with their past lives and habits, even after they have confessed Christ. Unfortunately, God does not see a hypocrite when He looks at a true believer, particularly when that believer has their focus fixed on God and is striving to be better. After all, He worked with Peter knowing he was hot-tempered and would one day betray Him.

It is good for all of us to start and finish well, but some of us may have started badly. However, finishing well is what matters, and that is what the grace of the eleventh-hour miracle is for. The Christian journey is all about remaining in His presence and allowing Christ to do that which was finished on the cross in our lives. It is a journey, and with time, we will see ourselves looking more like Christ if we stay put and allow Him to do His work in us and through us.

Many times, we think our emotions and personal efforts can make us better. Imagine when Peter assured Christ that he would go all the way with Him, even to the death. Christ Himself knew that Peter was incapable of doing as he had said, which is why He told Peter that he would deny Him before the rooster crowed. Christ knew Judas would betray Him, and He also knew Thomas would doubt His resurrection. Despite the shortcomings of these people, God still had plans to work with them. What matters most to God is that these people have a desire to see His will come to pass, despite their struggle with the flesh. He sees their future and knows that they will strive to be better once He empowers them with the Holy Spirit.

Consequently, that became the case, Peter became more gentle, bold, and able to show true leadership among the brethren. Thomas became more trusting in God and no longer doubted the words and promises of Christ. It is not God's desire that we fester in our past habits, as this has the potential to sever our relationship with Him and make us unworthy.

Matthew 7:21-22: "Not everyone who says to me, 'Lord, Lord,' will enter the kingdom of heaven, but only the one who does the will of my Father who is in heaven. 22 Many will say to me on that day, 'Lord, Lord, did we not prophesy in your name, and in your name drive out demons, and in your name perform many miracles?'

There are people who have shown genuine repentance following their personal encounter with Christ and have followed this up with visible actions. A good example of such a person in the Bible is Zacchaeus. This is what God desires, but it is not the case for many who have given their lives to Christ, as they stumble for a while before reaching maturity in the faith. Christ saw the need in Zacchaeus's heart, the humility shown by Zacchaeus in publicly climbing a tree, and so decided to visit Zacchaeus's home.

It takes more than just a need to attract God's intervention in our lives. God is always willing to intervene in our situations, but He is only able to make miracles happen where there is faith. It takes both a need and a willing heart (faith). If it were just a need, Christ would have healed everyone around Him. The willing heart represents a person who has the required faith to cause the miracle to happen.

(John 5:1-15) The man with infirmity for thirty-eight years was healed by Jesus at the pool of Bethesda in the presence of other sick people. Even though Jesus did not make an attempt to heal other sick people at this pool, the Bible does not record any attempt or request to be healed by others who witnessed this miracle.

Common sense tells us that if you heal a sick person in the midst of many other sick people, others would immediately want you to heal them as well, asking something like, "Master, what about me?" There was no record of this in the Bible. What I deduce from this is that Christ went straight to the only person whose heart was right to receive a miracle at that particular point in time.

## *Light in the Last Days*

Many in the Western world wear their hearts on their sleeves when it comes to religious conversations. They do not engage in such conversations with a fine-tooth comb because they consider the Bible to be an anecdotal manual for managing our lives and affairs in today's world. But I must tell you, the Bible is ever relevant in our world today because it has remained relevant from age to age and generation to generation.

Even though the Bible can't scientifically prove God's existence, I must tell you that science has proven God's existence, as well as the fulfillment of Bible prophecies right before our eyes. Yet, God is still perceived as the popular villain in the West, like an ongoing Hollywood script, with so much focus placed on the book of Deuteronomy, where the Bible talks about stoning a rebellious child and an adulterous person.

The world is throwing everything it has in its arsenal, including the kitchen sink, at Christians just to stop the good news, but it has failed so far, just as they failed in the days of the apostles. In Luke 5:17, we see the faith exercised by four friends and how they passed their friend through the roof just to get to Jesus. Christ then said the sick man's sins were forgiven, only to be criticized for that. Remember that the world we live in is mixed with both believers and critics, just as it was in the days of Jesus. Yes, there are critics in the house, but this has not stopped those who needed to exercise their faith in Christ from doing so.

A man of God once said, if you spend time around people of faith, you'll catch the "faith fever," but the opposite happens when you mostly surround yourself with critics of the faith. There will always be critics of the faith in our midst, but our focus should remain on Christ, where our salvation and the power to change our destiny lie. Also, despite the state of decay we see today, please remember that there are committed Christians still on fire for God, in what we might describe as a fallen world. Just know that you are not alone in this journey, keep fighting the good fight and doing your work of faith.

It is also never helpful to see some Christians taking sides with the world and assuming the position of a judge over God's moral conduct. They are quick to refer to the Old Testament, specifically to Leviticus 20:10-12, where the law of Moses sanctioned stoning an adulterer and the adulteress, and Deuteronomy 21:18-21, which also sanctioned stoning a stubborn and rebellious child.

God's inability to behold sin might be responsible for some of the harsh laws in the book of Moses, and God Himself has made efforts to remedy this by bringing Christ between Himself and mankind. Those castigating the Bible over Deuteronomy 21:18-21 and Leviticus 20:10-12 seem to have lost sight of the message of love preached by Christ.

Unfortunately, we are not in a position to decide for God because God does not take instructions from us. We can sway Him, by asking for His mercies, to make Him change course on certain decisions, but we can't order God around. (Abraham pleaded with God for Lot's sake, Genesis 18:16-33; the Lord gave King Hezekiah fifteen more years, Isaiah 38).

I remember when my eldest son was just about a year old. Every evening at about 5 p.m., after I arrived from work, I would carry him on my shoulder and walk into the garden to give him a glimpse of what goes on beyond our fence. I did this daily, just to make my son happy. Most times, he took charge of the TV, watching his favorite channels. My one-year-old child cannot forcefully order me around or make me take instructions from him, yet I am happy to go out of my way just to see him smile. I would try to please my son because I love him. I am certain this is not peculiar to me, but something most parents do for their kids.

So, too, is our relationship with God. We cannot force God to take instructions from us or make Him please us. But just as earthly parents, God will go out of His way to fulfill our needs just to see us happy. God's instructions to the Israelites, to leave a bundle of grain and not go back to it, so the widows, the fatherless, and even foreigners can have something for themselves (Deuteronomy 24:19) show an understanding Father who cares. This is in sharp contrast to the malevolent God that many atheists describe.

It is understandable that most of these liberals have been sold a lie by the devil, that people can live a fulfilled life without God. Unfortunately, they fail to understand that there is no vacuum in the spirit realm. If you are not for God, then you are automatically enrolled into the camp of the devil, even without your permission.

Come to think of it, God is God and will remain God, no matter what we think of Him. When we praise and worship Him, we are not reminding Him of who He is. God already knows who He is better than anyone else, and He knows He is God. He knows He is the Almighty, and He knows He has the final say. Therefore, when we worship God, we are only acknowledging that we know He is God and we are honoring Him with our reverence.

God was there at the beginning. In fact, He began the beginning and created the world. He watched your great-grandfather as a helpless little baby when he was born, until it got to your father's turn. He watched your father as a helpless little child when he was born, and He watched you as a helpless little child when you were born. He will be there when you grow old, grey, and frail. If Christ tarries, your children will require God's mercy, and He will also witness your funeral, as well as those of your descendants. Considering these facts, what makes us think we can set the rules for God? He sets the rules, and we are bound to follow. Despite God's Almightiness, He is still a gracious God who accommodates our mistakes with second chances and plenty of opportunities for a fresh start. All He's asking of us is to work towards perfection.

# CHAPTER TWENTY-ONE

## *God's Last Move*

If many of us can cast our minds back to some precarious situations in our lives when all hope seems lost, and there was a sudden twist of fate in what can be described as unexpected help. We will start this chapter with a story by Charles Morris in February 2021, titled "Checkmate."

"There is a painting that once hung in the Louvre museum in Paris, painted by Friedrich Moritz August Retzsch. Today, the painting is popularly known as "Checkmate." It is now in private hands, having been sold in a Christie's auction in 1999.

The painting depicts two chess players. One is Satan, who appears arrogantly confident. The other player is a man who looks forlorn. If Satan wins, he wins the man's soul. You can view more of the creepy details below.

## The Chess Grandmaster's Discovery

According to legend, and probably fact, the story goes like this. A chess grandmaster came upon this intriguing painting in the Louvre museum alongside other famous art such as the Mona Lisa.

*Light in the Last Days*

The grand master stared a long time at the chess board in the painting and finally noticed something surprising. The typical interpretation of the painting (that the devil had the man in "checkmate") was incorrect.

Though the devil seemed to be the obvious victor, he was in fact not winning. The man, who thought he was losing, was actually winning.

According to the arrangement of the pieces left on the chess board, his king had one more move. This fateful move would make him the winner of the game.

The grand master called the curator and determined that the title "Checkmate" did not fit the scene because the forlorn-looking player actually had the ability to defeat his opponent, though he didn't realize it yet. His king had one more move.

Charles Morris proceeded to talk about the spiritual implications of this painting, in relation to what the grandmaster discovered. He said, repeatedly in Scripture, God assures his people that there is always a way of escaping situations that seem hopeless at the time.

When Goliath terrorised the children of Israel for 40 days, leaving the Israelites scared to death, and hopeless. Goliath was on top of the world, and he had no idea that God had got one more move in the person of David.

When the Israelites lost the ark to the Philistines in battle and the glory of God departed from Israel, and the Philistines brought the Ark of Covenant to Dagon as a trophy, they had no idea that God had one more move.

The bible said Laban repeatedly changed the terms of his agreement with Jacob, he did this ten times, just to cheat him out of his fair share of the livestock, Laban had his way, until God made the final move that resulted in Jacob having the upper hand.

When the Chaldeans thought they had conquered the Israelites and took away the gold and silver wares from the temple of God as a trophy, they had no idea that God had one more move. They only saw God's move on the day they used the cups to drink.

The three Hebrew Children, Shadrach, Meshach and Abednego were thrown into the fiery furnace. The King did the worst that he could to these boys by attempting to roast them alive, but God made the last move by ensuring the king does not have the final say on this matter.

When Joseph's brothers thought they had ended his dreams by selling him off to the Egyptians, they had no idea that God had one more move through Pharaoh's dream.

When the devil sowed the seed of disobedience in Esau, the heir, and made him marry those Edomite women, corrupting the blood line against God's instructions. The devil had no idea that God had one more move in the person of Jacob.

## Light in the Last Days

When Pharaoh took Sarah from Abraham, in what was clearly a hopeless situation, Abraham himself had no idea that God had one last move.

When the devil used Judas Iscariot to sell Christ and got Him crucified, the hope of redemption was crushed but the devil has no idea that God has one more move, which was Christ's resurrection. I suppose this story might be of help to someone.

This is a true story about my dad, Patrick Ossai, and I am telling this story because it might encourage someone looking up to God to come to their rescue.

When my dad was a young man, a bachelor, sort of. He was known to be a very sociable person, some kind of Socialite. He was known to be a good dancer, high life, ballroom dance, name it, and that earned him the nickname Oslow Papa.

At the time, he was just a Seaman working aboard a ship. They would go on tours that lasted about 3 months, usually in the rainy season when the river level rises to its highest.

On one of such trips, at about 9pm at night when no one was with him on deck, my dad slipped and fell into the river. The ship was travelling on a double engine at a very high speed, making it quite impossible for him to catch up with the ship.

According to him, it would be impossible to swim to either side of the river amidst the darkness, coupled with the fact that river Niger is a big river and the river has extended by over a kilometre on either side, due to the rainy season. This means he might not make it, if he attempts to swim to the shore.

He said he just thought to himself, to try as much as possible to stay afloat, hopefully, the crew of the ship will realise he was missing and come in search of him. Before he knew it, the ship was now about kilometres away, and continued without stopping.

Most of his peers were in the common room, relaxing and listening to the radio as the DJ entertained them. In a sudden twist of fate, a track my dad loves so much began to play, and obviously, his peers associated this song with him. Suddenly, they began saying to one another, this is Oslow Papa's song, get him to give us those dance moves. They did not stop at just saying this, they went to his cabin but he wasn't there, and then went to the deck and looked around, he wasn't there either. The urge to get him to show off his dance moves did not abate, they then went to other parts of the ship to see if they could find him, and he wasn't there, that was when it dawned on them that Patrick Ossai was missing. They immediately alerted the captain and a quick thorough search of the ship was conducted and they could not find him.

The captain of the ship immediately turned the vessel around. To ensure maximum visibility on the water from a distance, they turned the ship's navigation lights to full brightness, as they provided the strongest light output, allowing them to see anything on the water from afar.

They travelled close to 20 minutes, looking out and calling out his name, until they got to a point where they saw something looking more like a football on the water, that was his head above the water as he was still trying to stay afloat. They eventually got to him, threw a line to him and fetched him out of the water.

Normally, they would have said, "I wish Oslow Papa was here, he would have shown us his dance moves one more time." But this time, they didn't. They wanted him to actually come and show them the dance move.

Funny enough, this was a radio programme, and it never occurred to these men that by the time they got to his cabin to fetch him, the track would have finished playing. Something unexplained was driving them to go get Oslow Papa, not just one of them, but all of them in the common room wanted him to demonstrate that peculiar dance move. This collective desire led to the urgent need to go searching for him.

*Light in the Last Days*

Unbeknownst to them, Oslow Papa was fighting for his life, trying to stay afloat and hoping his colleagues would notice he was missing. That was God's one last move.

The devil thought he had my dad that day, if my dad had died, I would not have been born. The devil had his way until God made his last move, which was to make the radio station play a track that would provoke my dad colleagues to have a need for him. Of all the songs in the world, how the radio station picked this particular song at a time it mattered most remained a mystery, this shows God is never late when He makes His last move.

The devil may have gotten you where he wanted, he may have pushed you into depression, fornication, adultery, stealing, gambling, cheating, murder, cultism, anger, unforgiveness, bitterness, shame, and you are saying "God, I don't want to be like this, but I am helpless."

I want you to know that God has one more move to help you. All you need to do is raise your hands in surrender to Christ, and in a twist of fate, something will happen that will rescue you from that situation.

You might feel trapped, or you might be someone in a cult or in Hollywood already enlisted as one of Satan's end-time agents, thinking you will have a free ride in shutting down the Christian faith. I want you to know that God still has one last move once you have done your worst. Just as many who did their worst only to realize God had beaten them to it, I would encourage you to focus your strength on God, the one who has the last move and the final say.

# CHAPTER TWENTY-TWO

## *Pursuing a Life of Purpose*

Our God-ordained purpose is the primary essence of our sojourn on earth. It should be at the center of our lives, with every other aspect aligned around it. Our relationships, choice of spouse, career path, and even the city we choose to live in are all secondary, as they should be determined by our life's purpose. This purpose is the driving force and the key determinant of what, and who can be taken on board our journey through life.

Some of us might be tempted to argue that we spent our whole lives attending to our family's needs and, in the process, forgot about our own life's purpose. This often happens when we come to the realization of our purpose after other elements of life are already firmly in place. For those who still feel compelled to pursue their purpose at that point, it may require dismantling an existing structure. This can sometimes create tension in the home and in marriage if not managed wisely.

It is important to understand that each of us has a unique purpose. What God has called me to do is different from what He has called my son to do. My son might be connected to my vision, but the dimension of his walk with God will be distinct. The people I am meant to impact and the method through which

I do so will differ from those of my children. Each of us is unique, with different callings, playing different roles in God's plan.

God does not expect us to abandon our families. After all, the Bible places a strong emphasis on family before service, encouraging us to care for our households before taking on roles in the church. As 1 Timothy 3:5 says, "For if a man know not how to rule his own house, how shall he take care of the church of God?"

That is why it is crucial to place our purpose at the center of our life's journey. Our choice of career and spouse should flow from that purpose. When we align our lives this way, our jobs or family responsibilities will not choke the purpose God has given us.

When He gives us a purpose, He also makes provision for its fulfillment. But that provision often only becomes available after we take those first steps of obedience to pursue it. God will not allow your family to suffer. He provided bread for Elijah during a long journey, and He ensured that manna continued to fall from heaven for the Israelites even after they entered the Promised Land, until they had grown their own food and were ready for harvest.

Many who discover their purpose and begin pursuing it before choosing a spouse have a higher tendency to succeed than those who do otherwise. A friend who recently gave his life to Christ was sharing a conversation he had with his fiancée.

He was returning home from church with a smile after one of the Sunday services, clutching his Bible as he stepped out of his car, only to be greeted by the frown of his highly irritated fiancée, who was waiting for him in front of the house.

She immediately gave him a stern warning, saying she was only tolerating his church attendance for now because they were not yet married. However, she made it clear that once they got married, "this church thing" would have to stop. Interestingly, they already had plans to visit the council to pick a wedding date, as they were quite close to tying the knot.

He knew she meant what she said, he told us she's not the kind of person who bluffs, so he decided not to take her words lightly. Funny enough, his efforts to bring her into the faith were met with stiff resistance. That warning bell prompted him to take decisive action and end the relationship. In his words, "What I need now is someone who will draw me closer to God, not someone who will pull me away from my newly found faith in Christ."

He admitted that his fiancée was a very nice girl, but they hadn't been going to church when they first met, and now, introducing faith into their relationship had become too much for her to accommodate. Unfortunately, this is often the result when we choose a spouse or a job before embracing our God-ordained purpose. Our purpose can easily be choked, especially when the spouse or job views it as an inconvenience.

If we discover our purpose and place it at the center of our lives, then we are more likely to find a job that allows the purpose to flourish and a spouse who will help us realize it. Of course, there are several examples of people who discovered and pursued their purpose after marriage and still succeeded. However, many marriages have struggled when either the husband or wife suddenly began to go off tangent, following a new revelation from God for their life.

## God Is Our Great Reward

We will now consider the role of God as our Great Reward in our walk with Him, and how this brings about the fulfillment of purpose and destiny. Destiny is God's purpose for our lives. It is God-centered and a reflection of the Creator's intention for His creation. This intention preceded our creation. Therefore, God's purpose for our lives is pre-planned. The Bible says that a thousand years on earth is like a day in the sight of God. He is the One who knows our end from the beginning.

Beyond our happiness, good health, prosperity, or having children, God's primary intention for creating man is for His glory. How He chooses to involve us in fulfilling that purpose and bringing glory to His name is entirely up to Him.

Many people define destiny in vague or superficial terms, often focusing on things that are fleeting. But these types of destinies do not endure. Nothing is critical to our survival except God. The people we love can fail us. Our health can fail. Our investments can be wiped out overnight. And in the midst of all this, God remains our only true hope.

Heroes of the past are now often recast as villains, their record of good in their days now seen as an abomination in our day. This should be a lesson for anyone striving to make history or a name for themselves. We must realize that nothing built on sand will last. That's why I like to say, Let's build on the unshakable Rock. Let's build on God. That's the only legacy that will endure. As God said in Genesis 15:1, "I am your great reward."

It is interesting to see Zerubbabel's name mentioned in the genealogy of Jesus Christ. Zerubbabel was a Jewish leader and a Persian-appointed governor who was chosen by God to rebuild the temple (Ezra 3:1–13). It is one thing to be chosen by God, and another to submit to His will. In Zerubbabel's case, he submitted. Therefore, it comes as no surprise that God honoured this obedient man by including him in the lineage of Jesus. To this day, many Christians reference Zerubbabel in their prayers, especially when praying for the grace to finish well. Zechariah 4:9 reads, "The hands of Zerubbabel have laid the foundation of this house, his hands shall also complete it."

Today, it's not Zerubbabel, Joseph, or David, it's you who is on stage. Now is your time to submit to God's will. And just like Zerubbabel, you may not be alive to witness the full impact of your obedience, but your name can endure for generations to come.

I would like to dedicate this paragraph to our young people, those who have the world ahead of them, yet face many crossroads and countless choices on the journey of life. Measuring true success has always been difficult, and it has become even more contentious in today's world, as the definition of real value grows increasingly vague. At times, vanity distorts our perception, causing us to see success through a limited and often misguided lens. We've frequently measured success by the wealth we acquire, the number of children we have, or the length of our lives.

Yet, according to Scripture, all of these are gifts from God. The power to make wealth comes from Him (Deuteronomy 8:18). Longevity is a promise of God (Psalm 91:16). Children are His gift, as Psalm 127:3 declares. The Bible, in part, describes Isaac's greatness through the wealth he acquired. God also blessed Jabez with wealth. Hannah, who cried out for a child, was blessed by God. And Scripture speaks often of the blessing of long life.

Therefore, it is not wrong for Christians to see wealth, children, and longevity as blessings, because God indeed promised to bless us with these gifts. It is possible to have all of them and still live a life of purpose and fulfill destiny, but this is not always the case. While Enoch was taken by God in his prime, he fulfilled his purpose. Meanwhile, his father, who lived longer, is not recorded as having fulfilled his.

Your purpose is not measured by someone else's. What matters most is that you do exactly what Christ has called you to do, no matter how insignificant that may seem. It's not about what we desire to do for God, but what God desires us to do for Him. That is what truly counts.

I don't know what's on your mind right now regarding the calling God has placed on your life. You may feel tempted to run from it just like Jonah did, choosing a different path or assignment instead. In one of his messages, Steve Eaves quoted Bill Johnson, who said, "When you avoid the battle you were born for, you'll face a battle you're not equipped for." Steve went on to illustrate this with the story of King David. David was meant to be on the battlefield, but he stayed behind and in doing so, he ended up seeing something he shouldn't have seen. That moment led to sin and opened the door to a new kind of battle, one that haunted him for the rest of his life.

Gideon didn't have to be as strong as Samson to be called a man of valour. David didn't have to dream dreams to become a ruler. Joseph didn't need to be a great fighter like David to fulfill his destiny. As long as you are walking the path God has called you to, your contribution in your walk with Him is not insignificant, it is just perfect.

In truth, a destiny that endures is not measured by wealth, children, or longevity. Many in our world today have all of these blessings, yet are walking in the opposite direction of their calling. They may believe they are fulfilling purpose based on their achievements, but God, the One who defines our purpose, may see them as far from their true destiny.

As a matter of fact, only God, the giver of destiny, is in the best position to determine which life truly fulfills purpose, and which destiny is actually achieved. Let me quote Pastor Sam Adeyemi's insightful explanation of purpose: "The melon should not tell the lemon how big it should grow, even though their names sound similar. If a melon defines success as growing to its own size, that definition doesn't apply to the lemon. Lemons are designed to be small but potent. You can be big and be big for nothing. Each of them is good for their size, and that is it."

The God who called you is the One who determines whether or not you've met the mark. Sometimes, God's purpose for our lives may be found within another person's vision, because divine purposes can overlap. The fact that your God-ordained purpose exists within someone else's assignment does not make your calling any less unique.

My wife, Nkem, often emphasizes that everyone needs a destiny helper. She points out that even Jesus, on His way to crucifixion, received help from Simon of Cyrene, who carried His cross when His strength failed. She also references the role Aaron played in Moses's assignment, the role Naomi played in Ruth's destiny, and the critical part John the Baptist played in preparing the way for Jesus.

Importantly, the role of John the Baptist in Jesus's ministry was a divine arrangement, John was positioned to announce Christ to the world. In addition to having helpers of destiny, timing also matters. The spiritual realm ensures that your destiny helpers come into your life at a specific time in your journey, at a time when their help will make the most impact.

According to Dr. Pastor Paul Enenche, no matter how much Elizabeth and Zechariah prayed for a child, John the Baptist would not have been born until it was close to the time of Christ's birth. This is because John could not be on the scene fulfilling his calling when the One he was to forerun had not yet been born.

We all have just one life to live, and there is no need to wait for others to test whether the pond will crack in the middle of winter before we attempt to skate on it. If God is nudging us, it is important that we take those steps. We must discern when God wants us to go and when He wants us to stay. God has called each of us, but we must understand when our purpose requires us to move, or remain where we are to fulfill His will. Staying is just as important as going, if that is what God has ordained.

It is crucial to be sure of God's intention for our lives before making significant moves, because going when God wants us to stay can lead to calamity. Conversely, staying when God wants us to go may result in a future filled with regret.

## Light in the Last Days

We are all different parts of the puzzle in God's grand plan. Fulfilling purpose and pursuing God's will for our lives should not be done through the lens of another believer's journey, but through the eyes of God. We must not take up assignments in the body of Christ simply because they seem noble or popular, especially if God is ministering to our soul that He never called or ordained us for such roles.

God is not the author of confusion. He gives us the grace to prosper only in the area of ministry He has called us to. It's also important to remember that God's purpose does not serve any man's ego, but His own. Therefore, fulfilling purpose is all about glorifying God, sacrificing for God, and dying to self.

In the late 1980s and early 1990s, the Church began to embrace teachings on self-esteem and self-confidence. While these attributes are not inherently bad, they tend to place too much focus on the self, which undermines the essence of our relationship with Christ.

Some might argue that we need self-esteem and self-confidence to function well as Christians. The truth, however, is that these attributes flow naturally once we are anchored in Christ. Most of the great men of God who impacted their generation did not specifically pursue courses on self-esteem or self-confidence. They simply opened their mouths and allowed God to speak through them.

Christ's disciples, who were once seen as unlearned and timid, were later described as bold, not because they gained self-confidence on their own, but because of their connection to Christ. Even Christ Himself was recognized for His boldness.

Our world today has taken it a step further, from self-esteem and self-confidence to the popular cliché: "I do what makes me happy," where everything must revolve around how one feels. While we are not called to put ourselves in harm's way or allow others to hurt us, the fruit of the Spirit teaches us that life should not be only about us.

This is a quote from Pastor Tony Wastall of Lifespring Church Wolverhampton. 'The greatest threat to Christianity, I'm not downplaying it. It ain't demons or the devil. It's individualism. It's independent believers who have no intention of connecting with the body of Christ. The whole attitude is: "**I do what I want. It's my life. Nobody tells me what to do. No pastor or church is going to dictate things to me. It's just me and Jesus. I only obey God.**" Sounds spiritual, doesn't it? "**I'm not doing what you say. I'm not doing what others say. I just do what the Lord tells me to do.**" Hmm. Well, according to my Bible, it says: "Do not negelect fellowshiping with one another." I don't need a special word when that word is already there in black and white.'

This mindset has destroyed many Christians and many marriages, because it fails to consider how the other person is impacted. Focusing solely on what makes you happy may come at the expense of someone else's happiness, while the place of sacrifice is pushed aside.

I would liken this to the actions of the Israelites in the wilderness when they demanded meat from God. Numbers 11:33 [NIV] says, "But while the meat was still between their teeth and before it could be consumed, the anger of the Lord burned against the people, and he struck them with a severe plague." God was capable of giving them meat and likely would have, if they had made their request in a more respectful and faith-filled manner. But they murmured and complained in a way that grieved God. They were focused solely on their desire for meat and ignored how their approach would affect God.

In a similar way, Jacob's pronouncements over Reuben before his death reflect how deeply hurt he was by Reuben's actions. Reuben, as the firstborn, may have believed he was exercising his position, but he lost that place in his father's eyes. He pursued what felt good in the moment, without considering how it would impact his father.

Pursuing purpose must not come at the expense of sacrificing what it means to be a child of God. If God has called you, then He will make the provision.

God's provision often arrives at a divinely appointed time. This is especially true when it comes to fulfilling your calling or receiving the people meant to partner with you in your vision. Timing is not accidental, it's essential.

Jesus, even as a child, understood His purpose. At 12 years old, He told His parents He must be about His Father's business. Yet, He didn't launch His public ministry until years later. Why? Because the timing wasn't right. John the Baptist had to first prepare the way, earning the respect of the people as a prophet. His recognition gave credibility to his testimony about Jesus when he declared, "Behold, the Lamb of God."

While many prophets in the past pointed people to God, Jesus came to point people to Himself because He is God. This was a truth the Jewish people found difficult to accept. Therefore, God in His wisdom arranged the timing so that John's ministry would precede Christ's, preparing hearts to receive the truth. God's plan is not random; it unfolds with purpose. Trust His timing, it matters more than we often realize.

For instance, when God gave Nehemiah the vision of rebuilding the wall of Jerusalem, He made the provision possible through King Artaxerxes. The Bible in Nehemiah 2:1-9 reads: "2 In the month of Nisan in the twentieth year of King Artaxerxes, when wine was brought for him, I took the wine and gave it to the king. I had not been sad in his presence before, 2 so the king asked me, "Why does your face look so sad when you are not ill? This can be nothing but sadness of the heart." I was very much afraid, 3 but I said to the king, "May the king live forever! Why should my face not look sad when the city where my ancestors are buried lies in ruins, and its gates have been destroyed by fire?" 4 The king said to me, "What is it you want?" Then I prayed to the God of heaven, 5 and I answered the king, "If it pleases the king and if your servant has found favor in his sight, let him send me to the city in Judah where my ancestors are buried so that I can rebuild it." 6 Then the king, with the queen sitting beside him, asked me, "How long will your journey take, and when will you get back?" It pleased the king to send me; so I set a time. 7 I also said to him, "If it pleases the king, may I have letters to the governors of Trans-Euphrates, so that they will provide me safe-conduct until I arrive in Judah? 8 And may I have a letter to Asaph, keeper of the royal park, so he will give me timber to make beams for the gates of the citadel by the temple and for the city wall and for the residence I will occupy?" And because the gracious hand of my God was on me, the king granted my requests. 9 So I went to the governors of Trans-Euphrates and gave them the king's letters. The king had also sent army officers and cavalry with me."

Moreover, when God called Moses, He made provision in the person of Aaron by appointing Aaron to speak on behalf of Moses, who had a speech impediment. God can make provision, particularly when that provision is not just to satisfy the desires of our flesh but to pursue His purpose. For example, God blessed King Solomon because he asked for wisdom to lead God's people, not for himself, and Solomon received more than he asked for.

## Confirming God's Call

It is important to note that seeking confirmation of what the Lord is saying must be done with an open mind and not with a mind that is already set. When we approach God with decisions already made in our hearts, we risk hearing only what we want to hear, not what He is actually saying. One of the great spiritual dangers we face is the subtle influence of the permissive will, that is, when

God allows something because of our insistence, not because it is His perfect will. The permissive will is often fueled by the desires of the flesh, ambition, comfort, validation, or fear. It can masquerade as divine approval, but there is nothing truly spiritual about it. It caters to our wants, not necessarily our needs or His purpose.

One key truth about God's will is that it unfolds according to His timing, not ours. We don't have the power to choose when things happen, but we do have the choice of how we use our time, to follow God's will or not.

Choosing God's permissive will instead of His perfect will can come with consequences. Jacob for instance, pursued God's permissive will and ended up marrying two sisters, a decision outside of God's ideal plan and it wasn't until he wrestled with God and was left with a dislocated hip that he fully submitted to God's will.

The consequence of Jacobs' struggles with God was apparent in his conversation, when he met Pharaoh, the first thing Pharaoh asked was, "How old are you?" Traditionally, the expected greeting would have been, "How are you?" Pharaoh may have asked about Jacob's age because of how he appeared, perhaps worn out, limping from his injury, and physically aged.

Even then, Jacob didn't simply respond with his age, whether 80, 90, or 120. Instead, he spoke of how difficult his life had been, possibly as a way of explaining why he looked the way he did.

One thing about echoes is that whatever we say returns to us. The same is true of our thoughts, especially when our mindset is fixed. Even when we seek answers from God, what we often hear is simply a reflection of what's already in our own minds.

Sometimes in life, what we hear are simply the echoes of our own thoughts, loud, persistent, and familiar. These internal voices can easily be mistaken for the voice of God, especially when they align with what we hope to hear. That's why discernment requires honesty, surrender, and quietness before God.

We must constantly ask: Am I truly seeking God's will, or am I asking Him to bless my own? True discernment happens in the space where we are willing to lay down our own agendas. It's in that place of surrender that we can distinguish between divine leading and self-driven desire.

Genesis 13:5-17 [NIV]. 5 Now Lot, who was moving about with Abram, also had flocks and herds and tents. 6 But the land could not support them while they stayed together, for their possessions were so great that they were not able to stay together. 7 And quarreling arose between Abram's herders and Lot's. The Canaanites and Perizzites were also living in the land at that time. 8 So Abram said to Lot, "Let's not have any quarreling between you and me, or between your herders and mine, for we are close relatives. 9 Is not the whole land before you? Let's part company. If you go to the left, I'll go to the right; if you go to the right, I'll go to the left. 10 Lot looked around and saw that the whole plain of the Jordan toward Zoar was well watered, like the garden of the Lord, like the land of Egypt. (This was before the Lord destroyed Sodom and Gomorrah.) 11 So Lot chose for himself the whole plain of the Jordan and set out toward the east. The two men parted company: 12 Abram lived in the land of Canaan, while Lot lived among the cities of the plain and pitched his tents near Sodom. 13 Now the people of Sodom were wicked and were sinning greatly against the Lord. 14 The Lord said to Abram after Lot had parted from him, Look around from where you are, to the north and south, to the east and west. 15 All the land that you see I will give to you and your offspring[a] forever. 16 I will make your offspring like the dust of the earth, so that if anyone could count the dust, then your offspring could be counted. 17 Go, walk through the length and breadth of the land, for I am giving it to you."

*Light in the Last Days*

In Genesis 13:5–14, Abraham's actions reveal his deep faith in God, his willingness to submit to God's will, and his unwavering trust that God would bless him regardless of the immediate outcome. By allowing Lot to choose first, even if it meant settling for less fertile land, Abraham displayed a profound trust in God's promise over visible advantage.

His decision wasn't based on what seemed best in the moment, but on the assurance that his future was secured by God. It can be said that God recognizes when we put Him first, and He often shows up to affirm that trusting in Him is never in vain just as He did for Abraham after his separation from Lot. When Abraham offered Lot the first choice and was willing to take whatever land remained, he was operating in submission to God's will, fully confident that his success depended not on the land's appearance but on God's provision and guidance.

"So, when you follow God, anything can happen. You never know who you will meet, where you will go, or what you will do. And the sooner you come to terms with that spiritual reality, the more you will enjoy the journey."(UCB, word for today).

Remember, God speaks clearly, but His voice often requires a heart that is quiet enough to listen and humble enough to obey even when the answer isn't what we expected.

Most great men of God can tell you specifically when God called them or when they received confirmation of His calling. Sometimes, another man of God might give you a message about what God is revealing to them concerning your life. However, this is not enough to act on unless God has confirmed it to you personally. Therefore, you will need to pray for God's confirmation.

This can also work the other way around, God might speak to you about what He has called you to do, and while you are still contemplating whether this is truly God speaking, He may use another man of God to confirm it. God's confirmation is sometimes necessary, as it gives further assurance and insight into the parameters of what He has called you to do.

God spoke directly to Samuel, sent His angel to speak to Gideon, Zechariah, Samson's parents, and Mary, the mother of Jesus, and confirmed these revelations to Joseph, the father of Jesus. To this day, He continues to give direction.

It doesn't matter how young Samuel was at the time, God established contact with him by speaking to him directly. "With this, Samuel had a one-on-one experience with God." Joshua did not take on the task of leading the Israelites to the Promised Land based on words of encouragement from Moses alone, he heard directly from God.

The point is, if we hear from God about our life's purpose, it will be much easier to return to God for guidance, particularly when our assignment runs into difficulties. This is because we can remind God of what was agreed upon at the beginning of the assignment. Moses reminded God of His promise to take the people of Israel to the Promised Land..in Exodus 32:9-14 [NIV]. "I have seen these people," the Lord said to Moses, "and they are a stiff-necked people. 10 Now leave me alone so that my anger may burn against them and that I may destroy them. Then I will make you into a great nation." 11 But Moses sought the favor of the Lord his God. "Lord," he said, "why should your anger burn against your people, whom you brought out of Egypt with great power and a mighty hand? 12 Why should the Egyptians say, 'It was with evil intent that he brought them out, to kill them in the mountains and to wipe them off the face of the earth'? Turn from your fierce anger; relent and do not bring disaster on your people. 13 Remember your servants Abraham, Isaac and Israel, to whom you swore by your own self: 'I will make your descendants as numerous as the stars in the sky and I will give your descendants all this land I promised them, and it will be their inheritance forever.'" 14 Then the Lord relented and did not bring on his people the disaster he had threatened."

Just like Moses, Joshua also returned to God to review his walk with God, when things become difficult after their defeat in the hands of the men of Ai. Joshua 7:7-17. If God sends you, then there is room to review your walk with Him as in the case of Joshua.

"As far as we are in the service of the Lord and in God's purpose, we should not be fooled into thinking we are not fulfilling our purpose because we are not doing exactly what someone else is doing. We all have different roles in God's plan, and that is the beauty of walking with God.

Joseph of Arimathea was a follower of Christ who showed up only after Christ's death, at a time when Christ's disciples were in hiding, and there was a need for a man of Joseph of Arimathea's status to request Christ's body. Even though Joseph of Arimathea wasn't recorded among Christ's disciples or apostles, he fulfilled Bible prophecy by burying Christ in a virgin tomb. Joseph of Arimathea may not have planned to purposely bury Christ in a virgin tomb, but things worked out that way since his tomb was new, and prophecy was fulfilled.

The fact that Elijah was at the forefront in his day does not mean God did not recognize the other seven thousand believers. Some of us have our roles as believers to show forth Christ in our place of work and in the different spheres of our lives.

We are all called, but some are given assignments that require a lot of sacrifice and a higher grace to accomplish, which explains why we all have different grace. It is important to acknowledge that just because some Christians are breaking new ground in their own area of calling, does not necessarily mean we should switch from what we have been called to do. Your unique gifts and talents are aligned with your calling.

Exodus 14:15 [NIV]. "15 Then the Lord said to Moses, "Why are you crying out to me? Tell the Israelites to move on." With the Red Sea in front of them and Pharaoh's chariots behind them, the children of Israel panicked. As devoted Christians, the expected inclination is to cry out to God when faced with difficulties. In this case, however, God's response suggests that He was displeased with the Israelites' outcry and sense of hopelessness. This is because God knew that Moses already had what it took to handle the situation. The very staff that had been used to perform all the plagues in Egypt was in Moses' hand, and all God did was remind him to use what he already had, the staff. When responding to an assertion that a witches' conference could not be stopped, Archbishop Benson Idahosa once said: "God need not waste His time when I'm here. I can handle this," essentially asserting that he could effectively deal with the situation. In the same vein, God wants you to know He's relying on you to represent Him in that matter, whether in your office, community, or family. He's relying on you because He knows He has already given you what it takes to do what is necessary.

*Light in the Last Days*

You are not too small for God to use, and your talents are also not too small for God to use." In the Parable of the Talents in Matthew 25, a talent was a large sum of money, roughly equal to 20 years' wages for a laborer, meaning that 5 talents would be equivalent to 100 years' worth of wages. Whether it's 20 years or 100 years' worth of earnings, the amount Jesus refers to is undeniably significant. However, the talents in the parable aren't just about money; they symbolize the God-given gifts and abilities entrusted to us. This suggests that the gifts we possess from God are equally significant and essential for fulfilling our purpose.

God never leaves us empty-handed. In Christ's parables involving kings or masters giving responsibilities to their servants before departing, the person representing Christ in these parables never leaves without first making provision.

In Luke 19:12–13, the master gave his ten servants ten minas to put to work:

"12 Therefore He said: 'A certain nobleman went into a far country to receive for himself a kingdom and to return. 13 So he called ten of his servants, delivered to them ten minas, and said to them, 'Do business till I come.'"

Likewise, in Matthew 25:14–30, the master gave five talents to one servant, two to another, and one to the third: "14 For the kingdom of heaven is as a man travelling into a far country, who called his own servants and delivered unto them his goods. 15 And unto one he gave five talents, to another two, and to another one, to every man according to his several ability and straightway took his journey."

Moreover, consider the story of the Good Samaritan, which symbolically represents Christ and a wounded world. The Samaritan gave the innkeeper money to take care of the wounded man and promised to repay any extra expenses upon his return. Just like in the other stories, the Samaritan representing Christ did not leave the innkeeper empty-handed.

If you are reading this and thinking you have nothing to offer, I want to assure you that the Master who asked you to "occupy until His return" did not leave you empty-handed. Perhaps you're just thinking about this the wrong way. Gideon felt the same, he saw himself as the least in his family and his clan as the weakest in all of Israel. But God saw him differently. He called Gideon a "mighty man of valour" because the strength required to fulfill the assignment was already in him.

The two fish and five loaves, and the little oil in the jar, all produced great results when placed in God's hands. When God intervened in the life of the widow of Zarephath through Elijah, the miracle of provision followed. God has His ways, and most of His actions are predestined. Our purpose is a function of God's calling and design, never a result of our perception or the opinion of others.

Don't be guilt-tripped into doing what God hasn't called you to do, because the provision may not come if God didn't send you. As Dr. Pastor Paul Enenche once said, "You cannot take your bulldozer into another man's farm."

If we pursue purpose based on our own perceptions or the expectations of others, we may end up working in opposition to the very calling God has placed on our lives. Moses and Saul both made that mistake until the grace of God found them and redirected them back into their true calling. We are all called to share the Good News at every opportunity. We've been sent into the harvest field to bring in the harvest. However, when you feel God's hand strongly restraining you regarding a specific move, it's wise to seek confirmation from Him before proceeding.

Faith is not about trying to help God by leaping into the dark. Faith is about hearing from God and then taking deliberate steps based on His word. God promised Abraham a child, but instead of waiting for confirmation, Abraham leapt ahead and acted on the promise prematurely, leading to the birth of Ishmael.

The story of the young and old prophets in the bible book of 1 Kings 13:11-25, is another example of why we need God to confirm certain moves when in doubt.

1King 13:11-23 [NIV]. 11 There was an old prophet who lived in Bethel. His sons came and told him the story of what the holy man had done that day in Bethel, told him everything that had happened and what the holy man had said to the king.

11 "There was an old prophet who lived in Bethel. His sons came and told him the story of what the holy man had done that day in Bethel, told him everything that had happened and what the holy man had said to the king.

12 Their father said, "Which way did he go?" His sons pointed out the road that the holy man from Judah had taken.

13-14 He told his sons, "Saddle my donkey." When they had saddled it, he got on and rode after the holy man. He found him sitting under an oak tree. He asked him, "Are you the holy man who came from Judah?" "Yes, I am," he said.

15 "Well, come home with me and have a meal."

16-17 "Sorry, I can't do that," the holy man said. "I can neither go back with you nor eat with you in this country. I'm under strict orders from God: 'Don't eat a crumb; don't drink a drop; and don't come back the way you came.'"

18-19 But he said, "I am also a prophet, just like you. And an angel came to me with a message from God: 'Bring him home with you and give him a good meal!'" But the man was lying. So the holy man went home with him and they had a meal together.

20-22 There they were, sitting at the table together, when the word of God came to the prophet who had brought him back. He confronted the holy man who had come from Judah: "God's word to you: You disobeyed God's command; you didn't keep the strict orders your God gave you; you came back and sat down to a good meal in the very place God told you, 'Don't eat a crumb; don't drink a drop.' For that you're going to die far from home and not be buried in your ancestral tomb."

23-25 When the meal was over, the prophet who had brought him back saddled his donkey for him. Down the road a way, a lion met him and killed him. His corpse lay crumpled on the road, the lion on one side and the donkey on the other. Some passersby saw the corpse in a heap on the road, with the lion standing guard beside it."

God gave the young prophet clear instructions. In verse 17, the old prophet deceived the young prophet by insisting that God had said the young prophet could eat in his house. Unfortunately, the young prophet who had received specific instructions from God should have returned to God for confirmation. If God has a hand in an assignment, He will not leave the parties involved in the dark.

When God sent Elijah to the widow of Zarephath, He had already spoken to the woman before Elijah arrived. The angel and the raven would not have brought bread to Elijah if God hadn't ordained his stay at the brook and the long journey that followed.

God also confirmed to Peter that He was sending him to the home of Cornelius. However, He didn't just give Peter a mission, He also addressed Peter's mindset about associating with Gentiles. Knowing Peter's reservations, God prepared him by showing him a vision and telling him that nothing He has made is unclean. This was essential, as God knew He was sending Peter to the Gentiles, and He first needed to change Peter's perspective.

Likewise, when God sent Moses to Pharaoh, He immediately sent Moses' brother, Aaron, on a journey toward him to confirm that everything was already prepared.

## Light in the Last Days

Christ commanded all Christians to preach the Good News, and this commission is not limited to missionaries, pastors, or priests. We must all do the work of our Father in heaven, but within the area of our calling. That way, our work will endure. We can partner with or support other believers, but this too must be done within the boundaries of our calling.

Uzzah was committed and dedicated. He wanted to protect the Ark of the Covenant from falling, but he wasn't supposed to be there in the first place. Taking on assignments we're not called into can lead to frustration, strain within the home, and difficulties with one's spouse or children. Furthermore, the wisdom and grace needed to navigate tough seasons might be absent, and the tendency to lose faith in Christ becomes much greater.

Moreover, God may remain silent in such moments, because He did not authorize the move in the first place. You cannot walk with God based solely on the grace placed upon another person. Such grace will help to a point but might not tarry. You need your own grace to walk the walk, because a journey with God is rooted in personal relationship.

This is what God told the Israelites as they prepared to enter the land He had given them. Deuteronomy 11:11 says, "But the land you are crossing the Jordan to take possession of is a land of mountains and valleys that drinks rain from heaven." The valleys can represent difficult times, tests of faith, and the nearness of God.

Therefore, the fact that God is involved in your assignment doesn't mean there will be no troubles. What matters most is that God is walking with you. Sometimes, He may even allow disappointments to guide us back to the right path.

Let's use David's circumstance as one of such examples. 1 Samuel 29 [NIV].

"1 The Philistines gathered all their forces at Aphek, and Israel camped by the spring in Jezreel. 2 As the Philistine rulers marched with their units of hundreds and thousands, David and his men were marching at the rear with Achish. 3 The commanders of the Philistines asked, "What about these Hebrews?" Achish replied, "Is this not David, who was an officer of Saul king of Israel? He has already been with me for over a year, and from the day he left Saul until now, I have found no fault in him." 4 But the Philistine commanders were angry with Achish and said, "Send the man back, that he may return to the place you assigned him. He must not go with us into battle, or he will turn against us during the fighting. How better could he regain his master's favor than by taking the heads of our own men? 5 Isn't this the David they sang about in their dances: "'Saul has slain his thousands, and David his tens of thousands'?" 6 So Achish called David and said to him, "As surely as the Lord lives, you have been reliable, and I would be pleased to have you serve with me in the army. From the day you came to me until today, I have found no fault in you, but the rulers don't approve of you. 7 Now turn back and go in peace; do nothing to displease the Philistine rulers." 8 "But what have I done?" asked David. "What have you found against your servant from the day I came to you until now? Why can't I go and fight against the enemies of my lord the king?" 9 Achish answered, "I know that you have been as pleasing in my eyes as an angel of God; nevertheless, the Philistine commanders have said, 'He must not go up with us into battle.' 10 Now get up early, along with your master's servants who have come with you, and leave in the morning as soon as it is light." 11 So David and his men got up early in the morning to go back to the land of the Philistines, and the Philistines went up to Jezreel."

The interesting thing about this story, for me, is seeing the hand of God correcting David's misstep, which was the reason the Philistine commanders rejected David's offer to fight alongside them against the Israelites. Imagine David in battle, killing tens of thousands of God's people. That would have been the end of David. He would have died in that battle. His destiny, the throne, and all that God had planned for him would have been shelved. Ironically, the Philistine commanders who rejected David might have felt proud of themselves for putting him in his place, unaware that God was using them to preserve David's future.

David was going through great hardship as Saul sought to kill him, and this led to a lapse in judgment. He was almost pledging his loyalty to the Philistines because of the protection he received from them, but God wanted David's undivided loyalty.

Another lesson from this story is that even though God miraculously intervened to save David from sabotaging his future, that didn't mean his actions were without consequences. It was David's poor judgment, his decision to align with the Philistines against Israel, that left Ziklag vulnerable and led to the Amalekites raiding the city. This, in turn, caused his six hundred loyal men to turn on him, ready to stone him (1 Samuel 30).

Even the best of us can make mistakes. But God sees our hearts and can help us in those difficult moments. David's heart was fully committed to God. Instead of fainting, he encouraged himself in the Lord and after inquiring of God, the Lord came through for him.

## A Destiny That Endures – Our Great Reward

Young people are often more likely to measure a fulfilled destiny in material terms, but material possession alone is not the measure of a destiny that endures.

Consider the story of Esau and Jacob. While Jacob was the blessed one, his brother Esau appeared to enjoy prosperity first. They were twins, two people of the same age and while Jacob was still single, Esau already had two wives. Apart from the well-known account of Esau being famished and exchanging his birthright for a pot of stew, there is no indication that he wasn't taking good care of his two wives. In their time, most young men would likely have seen Esau as the prosperous one and viewed Jacob as some kind of failure, especially if destiny is measured only in terms of wealth and children.

Many in their day might have seen Esau as creative, more active, more outgoing, and the one with the most potential, particularly if they ignored his disregard for God's instructions to the family and descendants of Abraham. Jacob, on the other hand, valued what his brother had and treasured God's instructions to their family. God said, "I am your great reward." This is what set Jacob apart and made him someone whose destiny would endure.

Consider the children of Israel (Jacob's descendants). While Joseph's brothers were owning livestock, tending cattle, and marrying wives, Joseph was stuck in slavery and later in prison. Yet he had God, the one reward that truly makes the difference.

Sometimes, the very people we look up to or envy, because of their wealth or status may actually envy us for the peace we enjoy in our lives, something they lack. As a child of God, when you look closer, you may find that what you have is exactly what those you envy are missing. You are not a failure, unless God says so. Our Father and Creator has set different destinies for each of us. Our callings are different, and our purposes are all designed to glorify God, even though the methods may differ.

Consequently, the greatest gift God has promised mankind is Himself. Wealth, children, and longevity are all additions to God's blessings. This explains why, at some point in our lives, God may place us in a position where these blessings, wealth, children, or even life itself, are put at risk, to test whether we will still choose Him above all.

Imagine God's demand for Isaac from Abraham, He wanted to see if Abraham would place the gift (Isaac) ahead of the Giver. Christ did the same with the rich young ruler, who sadly put his wealth, the gift, ahead of God, who should have been his ultimate reward.

The disciples of Christ turned their backs on everything. They denied themselves of wealth, many died prematurely, denied of longevity, yet they fulfilled their purpose in the sight of God.

We know of many celebrities in Hollywood checking themselves into rehab or going for counselling following mental breakdowns. They have the money, they have the fame, and in their own eyes, they have fulfilled their purpose. Yet, many of them suffer from mental health-related issues, which is an indication of the emptiness and void within.

Here's a quote from the popular Hollywood celebrity Will Smith on March 28, 2024: "But what happens is you just realize none of it can make you happy," he continued. "Once you've bought everything you want and there's literally nothing on earth else that you want to buy, I just wish that was a gift that everybody could have because there's nothing that material can do to satisfy you."

Another famous Hollywood celebrity, Cardi B, said: "Even though I'm happy, I feel like I was a little bit happier two or three years ago when I had less money." Money in itself is good and can meet all our physical needs, but peace, arguably the most important need, is transcendent and cannot be bought with money.

Here's one more quote from Dayana Mendoza, Miss Universe 2008: "My marriage failed, my modeling career didn't fulfill or define me, and nothing was working out. I was desperate. That's when I fell to my knees, surrendered, and asked God to take control. I saw His mighty hand guiding me, helping me, and showing me the right path." Arguably, Miss Universe is the height of fame any model could imagine. She had the money, fame, and connections, yet she did not feel fulfilled. Dayana gave her life to Christ in the midst of the chaos, got baptized, and in a sudden twist of events, she eventually married a pastor years later.

That hollow feeling, the one that leaves people constantly seeking happiness yet never finding it exists because they have left out the One who said, "I am your great reward," and "I have come to make you complete."

God's desire is for us to prosper and be in good health. The Christian faith is not about dressing in rags, living in penury, or going through life like the proverbial "widow of the parish." There's often a perception that Christians should only express themselves in a reserved, conservative way rather than with joy and enthusiasm. But who says a Christian cannot laugh, be happy, and live a life of joy?

The idea that Christianity is meant to immiserate people is simply not true. Moderation does not mean deprivation, rather, moderation is about not allowing our desires to become idols in our lives. Nothing stops us, as Christians, from driving a good and expensive car, living in a nice home and neighborhood, or marrying a very pretty wife or a very handsome husband.

Every miracle Christ performed was to showcase the glory of God. Christ emphasized that His miracle of raising Lazarus from the dead was to demonstrate the glory of God. Therefore, being controversial and unbearable as a person defeats the purpose of the fruit of the Spirit, as these fruits are meant to benefit others.

When the Bible tells us to love the Lord our God with all our mind and all our strength, it's another way of saying we should make God our ultimate reward. Some may feel that such love is too much to ask, that it's impossible for human beings. But the kind of love the Bible speaks of isn't forced or external, it's a love that comes from within.

To understand this better, consider the experience of a parent coming home after a long day. Picture a one-year-old child who hears the front door open and their parent's voice. No one needs to instruct this child to run to the door, the reaction is instinctive.

The love is so deep and pure that the child drops everything, their toy, their food and rushes to greet the parent with joy. Even if the child isn't yet walking or is feeling unwell, they somehow find the strength. You'll see children bum-shuffling or crawling as fast as they can, just to reach that door. That's the kind of love God desires from us, childlike, wholehearted, unreserved. It's a love that puts aside personal pride, logic, or convenience and says, "You, Lord, are my everything."

Imagine a wealthy man like Abraham, with just one child, being asked by God to sacrifice that child, just to see whether Abraham considered Isaac or God as his greatest reward in his walk with Him.

Unfortunately, we will not all play the same role in bringing God's plan to pass. Some may lose their lives, some may have their health impacted, some may have to turn their backs on wealth or their ability to create wealth. Others may suffer dishonor, or walk away from family, while some may enjoy great honor. In all of this, as long as the name of the Lord is glorified in accordance with the leading of the Holy Spirit, we can confidently say that purpose has been fulfilled.

God operates both on a short-term and long-term scale. He may have a 500-year, 1,000-year, 2,000-year, or even 5,000-year plan, but we each make our little input during our short time on earth to help bring His plan to fruition. Ananias was only mentioned briefly in the story of Saul in the Bible, but the role he played was critical, leading Saul to Christ and thereby contributing to the rich gospel we enjoy today. Ananias himself may not have known that Saul (Paul) would have such a great and enduring impact. In the same way, I encourage you to make your own little input; you never know how far-reaching your contributions will be in God's long-term plan.

God is the God who was, who is, and who is to come. Therefore, He is able to ensure that His long-term plan remains on course by making short-term adjustments. Such an adjustment was made when God chose Jacob instead of Esau, because He foresaw Esau's carelessness with his inheritance. Someone once said: "It is not enough to have faith in God; we must also show God that He can have faith in us."

Come to think of Esau!

If Esau had known the great role he was meant to play in God's redemptive plan for the world, specifically, being the ancestral line through which Jesus Christ would be born, he might have taken his role as heir more seriously. God wanted a pure bloodline and had instructed Abraham and his descendants not to marry from the surrounding nations, including the Edomites. But Esau disregarded this instruction. As a result, God had to bypass him in one of those short-term adjustments and choose Jacob instead.

The truth is, if we see ourselves as the keystone in God's edifice, we will not live our lives carelessly. Perhaps Esau had no knowledge of God's plan for the birth of Christ, which would come 1,800 years later. His perception of God's instruction was short-term, and he saw no harm in marrying the woman of his choosing. But for God, especially regarding the birth of Christ, this long-term plan could not be compromised.

God always shows us in part. Esau did not see the whole picture, and even the disciples of Jesus only knew in part, that's why they suggested that Christ should start His earthly kingdom after His resurrection. God is primarily interested in our obedience. If we are obedient with the first step, He will move us into the next.

As you read this today, please know that you have a part to play in God's long-term plan. All that is required of you is to take those first steps in obedience. He will divinely place helpers along your path. Some of these helpers will cross your paths only once, while others you may encounter more frequently. What matters most is that the puzzle of our lives begins to make more sense as we take those first steps in obedience and trust our future into His hands.

Ananias, the believer who led Saul to Christ was simply going about his day-to-day activities as a believer when he played a key role in Saul's transformation. The fact that Ananias was mentioned only once does not make his destiny any less significant than that of the Apostles.

We will conclude this chapter by returning to the story of Esau and his brother, Jacob. Esau was a blessed man by all standards, a man with over 400 men under his command, able to say to one, "Come," and to another, "Go," and they would obey. Even in his later years, Esau remained wealthy and had many people in his circle, a position any average man of his time would have prayed and fasted to attain. His father Isaac was great in his time, and Esau undoubtedly inherited much of that wealth.

Young people are more likely to measure a fulfilled destiny in material terms. But material possession alone is not the measure of a destiny that endures. Despite being in such a coveted position, Esau was a man whose destiny, as far as God was concerned, would not endure. Meanwhile, his brother Jacob, who might have been perceived as timid was the one whose destiny has endured to this day.

At least the nation of Israel is still standing today as a testament to that enduring purpose. So, where are the descendants of Esau? God said, "I am your great reward." Please choose Him. Everything else will fall into place, and your destiny will endure.

# CHAPTER TWENTY-THREE

## *Satans' End Time Army*

In the Bible, in the book of Ezekiel 11:1-25, Ezekiel saw a group of 25 political leaders at the east gate of the temple in Jerusalem. These 25 men were responsible for subverting the will of God in the land of Israel. The reference to the "gate" does not imply they were watchmen, rather, they were respected figures in society, mostly tribal elders, people whom others looked up to for counsel and wisdom. Yet, God called them the problem of the land.

God had to take Prophet Ezekiel into the spirit realm, because, possibly due to the philanthropy of these men, we might be mistaken in perceiving them as the ones moving society forward, rather than seeing them as the spoilers they were.

In a similar manner, in today's society, we have people who have made significant contributions to advancing our world. Some of them are not unlike the 25 men God exposed to Ezekiel, as they have dedicated their lives to subverting the will of God, not just in their own land but globally. These globalists, some of whom have made their agendas known, are working both overtly and covertly to remove God from human societies. Their first point of attack is the family, because if you destroy the family, you deform the child.

Consequently, the place of family in our society is now being relegated, and this is not limited to Western societies, though it is more pronounced in the West. The idea of building the Tower of Babel surely began with a few people who garnered support and eventually made others buy into their idea of building a tower that would reach God. Similarly, the anti-God agenda being pushed in Western societies is championed by a few liberal individuals working hard to remove God from the affairs of man, while at the same time making the idea of family a subject of ridicule.

The truth remains that what sets religions and cultures apart are their beliefs, moral values, and doctrines. Be it Christianity, Islam, Buddhism, Hinduism, Heathenry, or liberal societies with sex-positive values, what sets them apart is their belief, doctrines, and values.

In Genesis 13:12, the Bible tells us that Lot pitched his tent near the cities of the plain, close to Sodom, but not within it. However, as the story progresses, we find that Lot eventually ended up living inside Sodom. This suggests that the values he once held may have gradually faded, leading him to fully embrace a lifestyle he once kept at a distance. It's a reminder that what starts as mere proximity to worldly ways can slowly transform into full immersion, just as we see in Lot's life.

Plains are typically lowlands, and the biblical account of Abraham and Lot's separation implies that Lot was on higher ground when he surveyed the lush plain of Jordan. Abraham said, "If you go to the left, I will go to the right; and if to the right, I will go to the left." This indicates Lot looked down from a higher elevation when he chose the fertile but spiritually dangerous plain.

When God rescued Lot from Sodom, the intent was to restore him to a higher place, back to the kind of spiritual altitude he had shared with Abraham. But Lot pleaded to remain in a small town in the valley instead, believing it made no difference. As we know, that choice did not end well.

Today, someone may be urging you to step away from a lifestyle that does not honor God. But instead of making a complete turn back to Him, you might be tempted to simply switch to a different, yet still ungodly alternative just to appear changed. Lot did the same: he left Sodom but settled elsewhere in the valley, rather than returning to higher ground. That compromise led to further loss and sorrow.

Let Lot's story serve as a warning: partial obedience or surface-level change is not enough. God calls us not just to leave sin behind, but to rise to higher ground with Him.

What globalists do is break down these doctrinal and cultural barriers, saying it does not matter, and that everyone must behave alike. The Muslims must behave like the Christians, the Christians must behave like the liberal sex positive people, and the Hindu or Buddhist must behave like everyone else. They tell you it doesn't matter, even when they know it matters a lot, because the spirit realm operates based on strict principles.

Even though the bible stated God's preference for Jacob over Esau, God did not overturn Esau's position as the heir, until Esau did that which he thinks does not matter. Also, God said He will not take the kingdom away from King Solomon because of His promise to David, but said He will take the kingdom away from Solomon's son. Interestingly, God did not take the kingdom from Solomon's son, Rehoboam, until he said things he thought did not matter, which resulted in Rehoboam losing 10 kingdoms.

Another story that comes to mind is that of Elimelech, his wife, Naomi, and their sons, Mahlon and Chilion (Ruth Chapters 1-4). Elimelech was a Jew from the tribe of Judah, originally from Bethlehem in Judah.

*Light in the Last Days*

Due to a famine in Israel, he temporarily moved his family to the land of Moab. Unfortunately, this decision ended tragically, with Elimelech and both of his sons dying, leaving Naomi to return home empty-handed.

In Deuteronomy 23:3 (NKJV), the law of Moses states, "An Ammonite or Moabite shall not enter the assembly of the Lord; even to the tenth generation none of his descendants shall enter the assembly of the Lord forever." Many times, we hear phrases like, "Let the children be themselves" or "It's their choice who they fall in love with."

The truth is that God depends on us as parents to guide our children in making the right choices, especially when it comes to their choice of a spouse. This is why God was able to vouch for Abraham, saying He trusted Abraham to direct his children in God's ways (Genesis 18:19).

Some might argue that parents shouldn't force their children into a particular marriage, and that's a valid point. However, it's worth noting that the Bible does mention Isaac and Rebecca's disapproval of Esau's choice of wife, which is a contrast to the situation with Elimelech, where such a response is absent.

However, Elimelech knew that God forbade intermarriage with the Moabites, yet neither he nor his wife stopped their sons from marrying Moabite women. Moving away from God's people to a forbidden land was one mistake, but supporting their children's marriage to people God had prohibited was another level of disobedience. The Bible does not mention the parents expressing dissatisfaction with their sons' choice of wives, suggesting that they might have supported the marriages. While they intended to temporarily live among the Moabites, this did not prevent the calamities that befell them. In addition to their premature deaths, neither of Elimelech's sons had children during their time in Moab. While it's not uncommon for some to face difficulties having children, the fact that both of Elimelech's sons died childless speaks volumes, possibly in terms of God's disapproval. It's likely other Israelites also journeyed to Moab to escape the famine in Israel, but Elimelech's story stands out as one of darkness.

On the other hand, Ruth, a woman from a people considered cursed, chose to follow her mother-in-law, Naomi, to live among God's people, with the intention of being buried there. We know how Ruth's story ended, she became the great-grandmother of Jesus Christ. Ruth's journey from Moab to Israel represents a transition from darkness to light.

Though Elimelech's story is from the past, there are lessons for us today. Many Christians today may say that it doesn't matter if we live and behave like unbelievers, often justifying it by saying, "It's just me doing my own thing." The truth is, whatever God calls bad remains bad, no matter how we try to rationalize it as harmless or acceptable. Just like Rahab the harlot, Ruth chose God's people and God's ways, and her life was never the same again. As I often encourage others, being among unbelievers isn't meant for us to adopt their views or become like them. Instead, our association with them, as Apostle Paul wrote, should be aimed at making them better, drawing them closer to Christ.

No matter how challenging it may be, let us strive to surround ourselves with people who will help us grow in faith. It might require some Christian discipline, but it is always worth it.

When you think about it, have you realized that not everyone who lived in Sodom and Gomorrah at the time of their destruction was a native of those cities? Similar to what we observe in our modern world, visitors from all over the globe are present in major cities at all times, whether it's New York, Beijing, Johannesburg, Lagos, or London.

Many individuals from cities and tribes favored by God perished alongside the people of Sodom because of their association with them, people whom God had not approved. Those who died with the Sodomites were there for various reasons, trade, tourism, pleasure, or even intermarriage. But what mattered most was their connection to that city.

Similarly, during the night of the Passover, several firstborn visitors, natives of other cities, were in Egypt. These individuals were not Egyptians, the people whom the angel of death was sent to punish, but they were in Egypt by association and, unfortunately, found themselves among those destined for judgment. Additionally, some Egyptians who had migrated to other parts of the world may have returned home for a short visit, perhaps for a week or two, only to be caught up in this punishment. It is uncertain whether these returning Egyptians were unaware of the previous plagues or knew but chose to visit anyway. Regardless, those who were firstborn became victims of the final plague.

As Christians, though we have been fortunate to find Christ, returning to what God has condemned may not be wise.

For Christians today who may think embracing worldly things is harmless, remember that the devil told Eve, "You will not surely die," yet she eventually learned the consequences of defying God. Our God is a God of precision and purpose, and everything matters to Him, whether it's something as small as David's wife criticizing him for dancing before the Lord, or how Miriam and Aaron spoke against Moses. Crossing God's boundaries today might not result in fire and brimstone raining down from the sky, but it will show up in ways that can take away our peace.

When God says it matters, even if the world insists it doesn't, be assured, it truly matters. While a few of these globalists are known and vocal, at the forefront of the movement, many others, particularly a large proportion operate in the shadows, hidden from plain sight.

They are scattered across and remain unnoticed in government departments, pharmaceutical companies, college and university campuses, and even in churches. These shadowy individuals are the most dangerous because they are the hands used by those at the forefront to implement their policies and agenda. They are hard to spot because they often hide behind the excuse of virtuously pursuing diversity and a more inclusive society. They look for a handful of people with strong anti-God views and use them to implement their end-time agenda, eventually making those views mainstream. These views suddenly become government policies that everyone is bound by.

The world is fast moving toward a false consensus, where good is suddenly classed as evil and evil as good. Most of what we consider Christian values are now politically incorrect in today's world. There is no better time to raise our spiritual antenna than now. As Christians, we must be able to discern the times we are in, just like the sons of Issachar.

## *Light in the Last Days*

The fact that we live in a world where almost everyone is living a godless life does not mean our devotion to God should be taken any less seriously. God's commandment to mankind in Matthew 22:37 remains unchanged: "Love the Lord your God with all your heart and with all your soul and with all your mind." This command stands, despite many people going their own way and doing their own thing.

Whilst aboard the S.S. Ethiopia, which was loaded with hundreds of barrels of whiskey en route to Africa for her missionary assignment, Mary Slessor was quoted as saying, "Scores of barrels of whiskey and only one missionary." Just like Mary Slessor, who voyaged on an alcohol-laden ship and went on to become a famous missionary, you too can live in a society where people are turning away from God and still remain a faithful Christian.

When I was growing up, we lived close to a river. Our parents had a standing instruction that we were not allowed to swim in the river whenever we went there. There was always a punishment waiting for us at home if we disobeyed and swam. Sometimes, when we got to the river and saw other kids including our friends swimming, we were tempted to join them.

But the fact that most of the kids in the neighborhood were swimming and that we were tempted to join did not make our parents' instruction null and void, nor did it mean the punishment wouldn't follow. No, the instruction still stood, and our parents would act on it when we returned home from the river.

In the same way, God has given us His commandments, and He will act on them when our time on earth is over. Just as my parents did not come to the riverside to chase us around, God will not chase us around here on earth. He has already given us free will. But it is His desire that we do what is right and be reunited with Him in heaven.

It's understandable that people tend to go to the extreme when describing their difficulties, they often prefer to narrate the worst-case scenario and view God only through the lens of Deuteronomy 21:18–21. In today's Western media, all we seem to see is a toxification of the Christian faith and a caricature of God as some kind of angry old man in the sky, with a beard and a big stick, just waiting for an opportunity to strike people down for their mistakes.

Unfortunately, this is a gross misrepresentation and Saul's experience is a powerful counterexample. Saul's intentions toward Christians as he journeyed to Damascus were unthinkably barbaric, yet God encountered him, forgave him, and gave him a second chance. Despite such redemptive stories, the narrative of a malevolent God remains widely accepted.

Take for example, the story in 2 Kings 4:1–7 [NIV], where the wife of a prophet cried out to Elisha because creditors had come to take her sons after her husband's death. In verse 7, Elisha tells her, "Go, sell the oil and pay your debts. You and your sons can live on what is left." God could have stopped at just paying off the debt, but He went further, providing a lasting means for the woman and her sons to live on. This shows God's character of grace and provision, not condemnation.

I must confess that the demolition of Christian values today isn't due to the strength of Islam but rather the weakness of Christians. Too often, we pray from a sedentary position without putting our faith into action. Instead of praying, taking a stand, and trusting God with the outcome, we pray and expect God to do all the standing for us.

The rise of political correctness has functioned as a tool to silence Christians, gradually discouraging us from saying many of the things we once spoke freely and that is exactly where the devil wants us, too afraid to speak about our God because of potential consequences.

## Light in the Last Days

Therefore, Christians must not remain silent. We are called to stand up for our faith and values. Standing up, in this context, does not mean violence or taking to the streets, but rather remaining steadfast in prayer and consistently professing our Christian beliefs anywhere and everywhere, as long as we don't force our faith on others. "Where the battle rages, the loyalty of a soldier is proved." -Martin Luther.

Acts 4:18-20 "Then they called them in again and commanded them not to speak or teach at all in the name of Jesus. 19 But Peter and John replied, "Which is right in God's eyes: to listen to you, or to him? You be the judges! 20 As for us, we cannot help speaking about what we have seen and heard."

If we mirror what God showed the prophet Ezekiel with what is happening in our world today, we will see that even some respected church leaders are now involved. They've become mouthpieces for various anti-God movements, pushing secular agendas even within the church of God. The truth is, nonsense remains nonsense even when spoken by someone respected. Therefore, any view or idea that leads people away from the core message of turning from sin, accepting Christ as Savior, and receiving salvation is not God's message.

The spirit of discernment is crucial in our time because the enemy is no longer outside the gate, they are now within. The wolves are wearing sheep's clothing, and their sole purpose is to lead the sheep astray.

There have been countless movements and attempts throughout history to crush the Christian faith. We can trace this from the first attempt by the Pharisees to cover up the resurrection of Christ, to many subsequent efforts that have come and gone. Yet, no matter the conspiracy, no man, no nation, no worldview, and no movement has succeeded in extinguishing the Christian faith. From the time of Christ's death until today, the Christian faith continues to grow. As nations in the Western world persist in removing God from their way of life and their societies, other parts of the world, particularly Asian nations with much larger populations are rapidly embracing Christianity.

The Global West cannot continue pretending not to see the green shoots of revival. Instead, they double down on their position, claiming there is no God, or insisting that those who believe in Him should not take the Bible seriously. I liken the stance of many of these individuals to that of King Canute, who commanded the waves to recede, not realizing that the sea is too vast and powerful to be tamed.

This is God's warfare and God will not lose to Satan or his so-called progressive agenda. A recent article, written with pride, boasting about how American liberals "conquered the world," reflects the drastic departure from the Christian values that once defined the United States.

It is clear that we now live in a world where liberal ideologies are dominant. But there is no better time to obey the command of the Great Commission than now. This is the best time to be a Christian, and it is an honor to be counted among the believers. For those who feel overwhelmed by the moral decline in our world, whose voices have been silenced, please know that the Lord is doing a new thing. He is at work, and He is gathering His own.

Let's compare the times we are living in to Christ's encounter with the two brethren on the road to Emmaus, as recorded in Luke 24:13–35 (NIV). Their response in verse 21 reflects the sentiment of people who believed, yet had lost hope: "But we had hoped that he was the one who was going to redeem Israel. And what is more, it is the third day since all this took place."

They believed Christ was the Redeemer. They believed in the prophecies about His death. But they lost hope in the resurrection. They saw a helpless Christ on the cross. They watched Him die without resistance. They saw the Lamb slaughtered for the sins of others, but they did not see the Lion who would rise from the dead, having conquered death itself.

Suddenly, everything they had believed, all the prophecies about the Messiah, His birth, His suffering, and His resurrection, seemed far-fetched. This is why Christ rebuked them so strongly in verse 25: "How foolish you are, and how slow to believe all that the prophets have spoken! Did not the Messiah have to suffer these things and then enter his glory?"

And beginning with Moses and all the Prophets, he explained to them what was said in all the Scriptures concerning himself. Many professed and practicing Christians today have watched as society and governments, even in countries once called "Christian nations," make examples out of believers. They are now applying the policy of "punish one, educate a thousand," meaning that if you use one believer as a scapegoat, others will learn. The ripple effect has caused many to stop professing their faith or sharing the Good News with others.

In some cases, the church itself is cheerleading these movements, persecuting fellow believers in ways that are causing others to question everything. Some, who are not well grounded in the faith, now believe the church has deceived them, that the existence of God and the call to sincere devotion were all lies. But the Bible is clear, in the end times, some church leaders will play a role in assembling Satan's army.

"We are now witnessing the unification of governments pursuing digitization to individually identify and control citizens. Soon, it will become easy to exclude a person from society, not necessarily by imprisoning them, but by rendering them 'non-existent.' When the Bible mentions that those who do not submit to the rule of the Antichrist will be unable to buy or sell, I assure you, preparations are underway to make this possible. Test runs have already occurred. A few people have had this experience in the UK where all the banks will close a person's bank account and refuse to allow them to open one.

This issue prompted Britain's financial watchdog to intervene in August 2023, investigating why banks were blacklisting and debanking individuals over their political views. When did banks become the moral arbiters of our society? This situation seems to serve as a trial run for what is to come. Without a bank account, one cannot receive a salary, make transactions, or withdraw cash.

Governments are now promoting groupthink, insisting that everyone must think and act alike, any speech or thought outside the approved narrative is prohibited. As we observe the world advancing its agenda, Christians pray for divine intervention, yet it seems as though God is silent while the world marches on.

Some Christians, who once had faith in God, now appear to lose hope, feeling that the world has triumphed and questioning the necessity of sincere devotion preached over the years. This sentiment mirrors the experience of the two disciples on the road to Emmaus, who saw only a dead Christ on the cross and lost hope.

Pastor Henry Oleghe of Christian Life Center Thamesmead once advised Christians not to lose heart when the issues we pray against as believers gain momentum. He pointed out that these events are foretold to occur in the last days, and such prophecies must be fulfilled.

The collaboration of governments to control the populace is a prophecy unfolding. Now that these foundations have been laid and people censored, we are witnessing bold actions by these end-time agents.

We observe bull worship at events like the 2022 Commonwealth Games in the United Kingdom and the 2024 Paris Olympics. The display in the UK during the Commonwealth Games symbolizes the Tower of Babel and Baal worship. The Tower of Babel represents a challenge to God's authority, while bull worship signifies a siege on God's people.

Then the Paris Olympics went a step further by desecrating the story of Christ and His twelve disciples. This was followed by the image of the golden calf, something we, as Christians, recognize as a symbol erected when people turned their backs on God. Never before have we seen such a unified front of global leaders walking in the same direction, boldly revealing what they stand for and where they are headed.

Many Christians praying for change and asking for God's intervention may feel overwhelmed as they watch the world they once knew spiral out of control, with globalists marching boldly onward. These are brazen acts, and the messages they convey are not hidden. In that same Paris Olympics, we witnessed, for the first time, a competitor being banned simply for making the sign of the cross. The prophecies of the last days are unfolding right before our eyes. We should not wait for another "road to Emmaus" experience before our eyes are opened to the times we are living in. Something is clearly afoot, we must all be able to see the fox and the grapes.

Many believers may be tempted to think that since the Bible prophesied that, in the last days, the love of many will grow cold and many Christians will be deceived by the Antichrist, it's acceptable to simply follow the crowd, believing that God will understand. However, Matthew 24:12, where Jesus speaks of the increase of wickedness and the love of many growing cold, is not a justification for disobedience. It is a warning, not an excuse. Those who choose to go their own way will not escape the judgment reserved for such rebellion.

Judas Iscariot found himself in a similar situation. Having likely read the prophecies, such as those in Isaiah, he would have known the serious consequences of betraying the Messiah. Jesus even said in Matthew 26:24, "The Son of Man will go just as it is written about him. But woe to that man who betrays the Son of Man! It would be better for him if he had not been born."

Despite this clear warning, Judas moved forward with his plan, thinking perhaps that since it was already prophesied, he was merely fulfilling destiny. But prophecy does not absolve anyone of personal responsibility. Normally, when a person is confronted about a wrong they're about to commit, they would reconsider. Yet, even after Jesus openly revealed that one of the disciples would betray Him, saying, "The one who has dipped his hand into the bowl with me will betray me," Judas persisted.

In the end, after committing the act, Judas was overwhelmed with guilt. Realizing the gravity of what he had done, he found the burden too heavy to bear. Tragically, instead of seeking repentance, he chose to end his life, taking an irreversible path that led to eternal destruction.

Pastor Banke Olowoyo of Christian Life Centre reminded believers that just as we see the devil recruiting his end-time army, God is also actively fulfilling His plans and recruiting His saints. In recent years, many may be surprised to learn that several Hollywood celebrities have given their lives to Christ. Unfortunately, those who are the loudest in the media often serve the world's agenda, giving the false impression that Christ is not gathering His own.

Aside from well-known Hollywood Christians like Mel Gibson, Chris Pratt, Tyrese Gibson, the late DMX, and Jon Voight, there are others, such as Sylvester Stallone, Mark Calaway (The Undertaker), and Terry Gene Bollea (Hulk Hogan), who have also accepted the Lordship of Jesus Christ. Countless Hollywood figures, once living far from God, have now acknowledged Him as Lord.

## The Parable of the Wheat and the Tares

Matthew 13:24-30 [NKJV] "24 Another parable He put forth to them, saying: "The kingdom of heaven is like a man who sowed good seed in his field; 25 but while men slept, his enemy came and sowed tares among the wheat and went his way. 26 But when the grain had sprouted and produced a crop, then the tares also appeared. 27 So the servants of the owner came and said to him, 'Sir, did you not sow good seed in your field? How then does it have tares?' 28 He said to them, 'An enemy has done this.' The servants said to him, 'Do you want us then to go and gather them up?' 29 But he said, 'No, lest while you gather up the tares you also uproot the wheat with them. 30 Let both grow together until the harvest, and at the time of harvest I will say to the reapers, "First gather together the tares and bind them in bundles to burn them, but gather the wheat into my barn."

If you're currently involved in a cult or engaged in an ungodly lifestyle, know this: God sees it all. He is fully aware that you're immersed in something that does not honour Him and yet, in His mercy, He is still giving you the opportunity to turn away while there is time. On the day of judgment, no one will be able to say, "The devil made me do it."

In the parable of the wheat and the tares above, the tares did not plant themselves, they were sown by the enemy. Yet, despite being the devil's doing, the tares were ultimately destroyed. The master didn't spare them just because they were victims of the enemy's schemes. Likewise, when Christ returns to separate His own from the rest, no excuse will stand, not even blaming the devil.

Christ knows exactly where each of us stands and to whom we truly belong. Just as the master in the parable was fully aware of the tares growing among the wheat, yet waited for the right time to act, so also Christ patiently waits, but judgment will come.

This truth also brings comfort to those who have been wronged. If you're feeling like justice was never served, or that the wicked have escaped judgment, remember: God sees. The God of justice will, in His perfect time, make all things right. It may not happen in your lifetime, but rest assured, He will judge rightly.

The previous paragraphs about how the tares will be dealth with may seem strong, but they reflect exactly what Christ said we should expect at His return. When we consider the parable of the ten virgins, the parable of the talents, and other similar teachings, one message stands out clearly, the Master was unwavering and just when He came back. This reveals something essential, the door to forgiveness remains open only until His return.

It is never Christ's desire for anyone to be lost. The story of the Good Shepherd reminds us of how far He will go to rescue each one of us. Even now, as you read these words, Christ is still reaching out to you in love.

He is the embodiment of mercy when justice demands a verdict, and the expression of grace where the law could rightfully condemn. But these gifts, mercy, grace, and forgiveness are available only before His return. When He comes again, the time for decision will be over.

As you read this today, know that the so-called "supermen" of Hollywood, the tough guys, the famous women, the icons who've done it all, are now bending their knees to Jesus Christ.

As a Christian, rest assured: there is nothing wrong with being a Hollywood star. What matters is understanding that no amount of wealth or fame is worth selling your soul to the devil. There are several Christians in Hollywood who have stood firm in their faith. If fame is your pursuit, or if you long to be seen as a hero, remember that people like Sylvester Stallone, a hero to many boys, and Celine Dion, a role model to many girls, have embraced Christ.

*Light in the Last Days*

Your identity as a Christian comes before your celebrity. Your calling is to use your influence to bring people to Christ through your humility, your compassion for the poor and needy, and your public witness for Jesus. Yes, the powerful elites in Hollywood may sideline you, or label you as a recluse because of your faith, but it is a sacrifice worth making.

John 19:38-42 [NIV]. 38 Later, Joseph of Arimathea asked Pilate for the body of Jesus. Now Joseph was a disciple of Jesus, but secretly because he feared the Jewish leaders. With Pilate's permission, he came and took the body away. 39 He was accompanied by Nicodemus, the man who earlier had visited Jesus at night. Nicodemus brought a mixture of myrrh and aloes, about seventy-five pounds. [a] 40 Taking Jesus' body, the two of them wrapped it, with the spices, in strips of linen. This was in accordance with Jewish burial customs. 41 At the place where Jesus was crucified, there was a garden, and in the garden a new tomb, in which no one had ever been laid. 42 Because it was the Jewish day of Preparation and since the tomb was nearby, they laid Jesus there.

From the above chapter, we can conclude that both Joseph of Arimathea and Nicodemus shared a common trait, they were secret followers of Jesus. Pastor John Blackah provided insight into the profound act of bringing Jesus down from the cross. He noted that Joseph of Arimathea and Nicodemus, both esteemed and wealthy individuals in society, likely had servants at their disposal.

Yet, they chose to personally undertake the task of bringing Jesus down from the cross, removing the nails from His hands and feet, allowing His blood to stain their clothes and cover their bodies. This intimate act marked a transformative moment for both men. The cross changed them. From that point forward, they ceased to be secret disciples and became openly devoted followers of Christ.

Remember the words of Apostle Paul "For I am not ashamed of the gospel, because it is the power of God that brings salvation to everyone who believes.."

Brethren, once you've encountered the Cross, you can no longer be timid in your faith. The Cross is not merely a symbol of suffering; it is the definitive expression of God's love and the transformative power of redemption. Therefore, as believers who have encountered the Cross, we are called to embody this same boldness. Our faith should be evident in our actions, our words, and our unwavering commitment to the truth of the gospel.

"Everyone therefore who acknowledges me before others, I also will acknowledge before my Father in heaven; but whoever denies me before others, I also will deny before my Father in heaven." (Matthew 10:32–33).

I recently watched Celine Dion's new music video on YouTube titled "Bruised for My Sake." As someone who enjoys feeling the pulse of viewers, I scrolled through the comments. One, in particular, stood out to me: and it reads thus... "Carry the torch for the Lord Celine. You may not have many friends after this but the friendship with the Lord is sweeter than the friendship with the world because the Lord's love is certain and full of hope. First Bieber, then now you. Blessed be the lord!"

Many might continue to hold the erroneous belief that the Christian faith belongs to a bygone age, unbeknownst to them, people are coming to Christ in droves, even among those in Hollywood, because God is gathering His own. Please don't be left out. Don't be in despair, God is also recruiting the saints, just as the devil is gathering his end-time army.

It is obvious that people are now disillusioned and becoming hopeless in governments that seem to have prioritized global agendas over the well-being of their citizens. This has prompted many to turn to God as their only source of hope, as they are suddenly faced with the helplessness of their governments.

As you read this, please be encouraged and know that you are not alone. It doesn't matter how loud or active Satan's end-time army appears, God is still at work and recruiting His saints. Just as Elijah once thought he was the only one left during the time when Jezebel and the worshipers of Baal laid siege on the land, God reminded him that there were still seven thousand who had not bowed to Baal.

Our depiction of Satan's end-time army as a group of combat-ready soldiers in full military gear might be misleading. That phase of physical military confrontation will come, but only when the Antichrist has taken his throne. What we see now are businessmen, politicians, political bodies, and alliances pretending to make life better and safer for people, while actually demanding that people surrender their will and silence their voices.

These few individuals have suddenly begun using the machinery of the state to make laws and even go further to redefine morality, a kind of morality that calls good evil and evil good. Yet, they themselves are above the law and not bound by the same morality they impose. As Neil Oliver rightly puts it in reference to the debate between Machiavelli and the prince: they make the rules but do not live by them.

There has never been a time since Christ when the end-time prophecies in the Bible have become so vividly real. Many may think the prophecy about people being unable to buy or sell under the reign of the Antichrist is far-fetched, but it isn't. The structures are already being put in place.

What happened in the UK, where people were debanked over their political views, is just the beginning. Soon, it may be because of religious views.

Countries are rapidly transitioning into cashless societies. In London, for example, you cannot pay cash for public transport, most restaurants no longer accept cash transactions, and workplaces are not permitted to pay staff in cash. Most African countries are also adopting and implementing cashless policies, with a strong push underway to make these societies completely cashless.

It is important to note that the majority of those advocating for cashless societies do not necessarily have an end-time agenda in mind. While some are doing this as a means of bringing all cash transactions into the tax net, others view it as a fraud prevention measure or simply a step toward more efficient operations.

Even though many are going about this innocently, they are unknowingly facilitating the rise of a one-world government. In truth, some nationalist politicians are making efforts to hold globalists accountable and to resist the advancement of their anti-God agenda. Politicians like President Donald Trump of the United States, Viktor Orbán of Hungary, and Robert Fico of Slovakia, among others, are now considered irritants by globalists due to their nationalistic views.

These few nationalists may slow the movement down to some extent, but even if they succeed in extinguishing most of the flames of liberalism, the embers will remain, ready to be rekindled once these leaders leave office. Furthermore, they will ultimately be unable to stop the globalists' push for a liberal world order, because it is a prophecy that must be fulfilled.

My encouragement to you, as believers, is to hold firmly to your faith and not to despair. Take comfort in the fact that we are witnessing the fulfillment of the Revelation given to John about two thousand years ago. This not only confirms that the Bible is true, but also assures us that the rest of that prophecy, including Christ's return and the final judgment will also come to pass.

Isaiah 43:19 (Message Bible): "See, I am doing a new thing; now it is starting; will you not take note of it? I will even make a way in the wasteland, and rivers in the dry country." Taking a closer look at this verse, God asks, "Did you not see it?"

Why would God ask whether we see what He's doing? He asks this question because there is a real possibility that we might become so overwhelmed by the state of the world around us that we fail to recognize what God is doing or saying in the moment.

The two men on the road to Emmaus must have known of the prophet Isaiah's prophecy about Christ's triumphant entry into Jerusalem, His crucifixion, and His resurrection (Isaiah 53). Yet, they didn't recognize that God was doing something new. They allowed themselves to become consumed by what they saw, Christ crucified on the cross, helpless and dead. It never occurred to them that this was God doing a new thing.

They failed to notice that the temple curtain torn in two from top to bottom at the moment of Christ's death was something new. They overlooked the darkness that covered the land from 12:00 PM to 3:00 PM as a divine sign. They didn't pause to ask themselves, "Is God still in control?" All they saw was hopelessness and the appearance that God had lost.

Therefore, be of good cheer and know that we are on the right course. Since we have been privileged to witness the Bible prophecy fulfilled thus far, the rest of the prophecy concerning Christ's return will also happen.

So far, the Church of God continues to march on. It is perhaps like a runaway train moving forward without pause, without slowing down. In the end, God will destroy both Satan and his progressive worldview. 'The earth is the Lord's, and everything in it.' (Psalm 24:1)

Therefore, the truth remains that, in one way or another, the Christian faith will continue to thrive unless God does not exist, which we know is not the case. The Church is marching on, and no conspiracy could or will ever prevail against it.

www.ingramcontent.com/pod-product-compliance
Lightning Source LLC
Chambersburg PA
CBHW052018070526
44584CB00016B/1799